GALATIANS:
A PRACTICAL GUIDE FOR BIBLE STUDY

Copyright © 2022 by Brandon Gonzales

All rights reserved. No part of this book may be reproduced or used in any manner without the written permission of the copyright owner except for the use of quotations in a book review.

First edition: September 2022

Cover and Book Design by Calli Cox and Moneta

ISBN (Paperback): 979-8-432-23739-2

Scripture quotations are from The ESV® Bible (The Holy Bible, English Standard Version®), copyright © 2001 by Crossway, a publishing ministry of Good News Publishers. Used by permission. All rights reserved.

ESV Text Edition: 2016

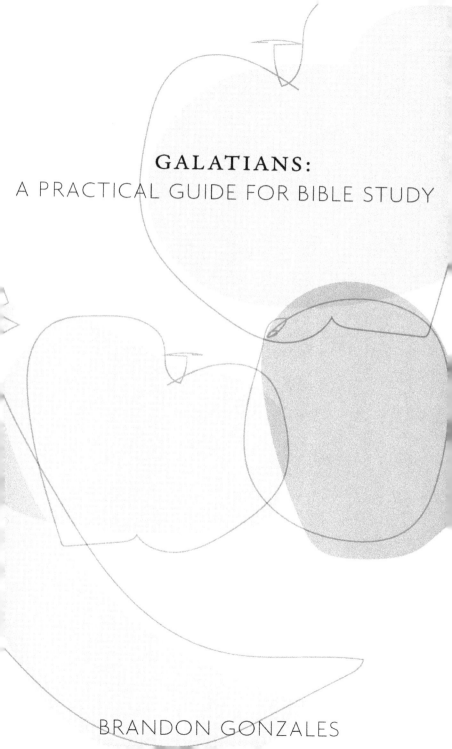

GALATIANS:
A PRACTICAL GUIDE FOR BIBLE STUDY

BRANDON GONZALES

To Aleia,
whose love and dignity
continually surpass my estimation.

CONTENTS

Acknowledgments
Introduction
1. A Greeting | Galatians 1:1-5
2. Curses | Galatians 1:6-10
3. The Former Murderer | Galatians 1:11-21
4. Paul Is Accepted | Galatians 2:1-10
5. Facing Hypocrisy | Galatians 2:11-14
6. Justification by Faith | Galatians 2:15-21
7. Bewitched | Galatians 3:1-9
8. A Criminal's Death | Galatians 3:10-18
9. Unity in Christ | Galatians 3:19-29
10. Laboring in Vain | Galatians 4:1-20
11. Children of Promise | Galatians 4:21 - 5:1
12. The Hope of Righteousness | Galatians 5:2-15
13. The Fruit of the Spirit | Galatians 5:16-26
14. Bear One Another's Burdens | Galatians 6:1-18

ACKNOWLEDGEMENTS

Throughout the months of writing this book, there have been those who took on active and critical roles to bring this work to your hands. Without their assistance and encouragement, this guide would have never been published.

First, I would like to thank my colleagues, Calli Cox and Moneta, for lending their talent in design. Your diligent labor helped make this small goal of mine come to fruition and I know many will be impacted by it. I pray the Lord will bless you both ten-fold.

I must also thank my parents for their loving support and encouragement. It is because you both taught me the importance of putting the Lord first that I am where I am today. Your inheritances are beyond this world.

To my grandparents, for your behind-the-scenes prayers that do not go unnoticed. I am so grateful for your love.

To my pastors, Mario and Arlene Villa, for your heartfelt care, counsel and service. Great are your heavenly rewards.

I cannot express enough gratitude to my fiancé, Aleia, to whom this book is dedicated. Your encouragement and words of affirmation never cease to inspire me. I'm so glad I get to do life with you.

To my aunts, uncles, cousins, nina and tia nina, who have inspired me to push beyond my boundaries.

To my church, for your hearts. May the Lord make his face shine upon you and give you the freedom of his Holy Spirit.

INTRODUCTION

Galatians is known as the Magna Carta of Christian liberty—the church's Declaration of Independence. Before Christ, God had instituted the Law to ensure that his elect people of Israel would remain pure as they dwelled among sinful nations. The Law, or Torah, with its myriad rites and ceremonies, placed restrictions on God's people. While it was pure and holy in its content, this body of 613 commands was never intended to save anyone. Rather, its sole intention was to illuminate the sinful state of humanity, notifying us of our desperate need for a perfect Savior.

Prior to the Mosaic Law was the Abrahamic covenant. In this oath, God promised the patriarch that he would make a great nation out of him. Though Abraham was old and childless, he trusted that our Father would fulfill his promise. It was through this covenant that Abraham believed in the Lord, and that very belief was credited to him as righteousness (Gen. 15:6).

From the story of Abraham, we learn that it was God's providential plan to save humanity by the gospel of grace all along. This will be a motif repeated throughout the book of Galatians. The gospel was not God's plan B if the Law failed to do its supposed saving work. The gospel was always plan A.

By means of his first advent, Christ came to dwell among us, fulfilling this Law that we could never fulfill, living according to the standard we could never live up to and satisfying the wrath of God that no amount of sacrificial lambs could ever satisfy.

INTRODUCTION

Such fundamental truths as these were being twisted in the Galatian churches. Now, as modern-day believers, it is our duty to understand how these truths were altered and how we can defend our churches against such blatant heresy.

The book that you are now holding will serve as your roadmap to this most excellent epistle. As opposed to being a distant narrator, I will be your tour guide, helping you along the way and providing personal insight. Any letter from the New Testament is absolutely glorious, radiating our Lord's luminous majesty for all of the Scripture's readers to revel in. Galatians so effectively displays this majesty given its primary focus: the gospel of Jesus Christ. And it is this gospel that is nearly impossible for us to grasp with our tiny, feeble minds.

If you are reading this book, then I would assume you desire to observe all that the gospel has for you. You are like an observer, standing at the edge of the sea hoping to capture its vast expanse; yet, in gazing at the sea, you may miss the little things occurring in the scene around you. Therefore, my job as your guide is to sit by you, taking note of the sand at your feet, pointing out the birds flying overhead and tallying each crashing wave, so that when you take your second glance you may observe all that God has created.

This gospel we endeavor to exposit is wider than our widest oceans; it is deeper than our deepest valleys; it is taller than our tallest mountains. It is my joy to help you embrace it all. So, let me tell you how to use this book.

INTRODUCTION

USING THIS BOOK

On a weekly basis, I host one-on-one Bible studies with my spiritual mentee. He and I have worked through numerous biblical passages, expositing them and faithfully applying them to our lives. In the midst of bustling local coffee shops, we have consulted various resources, both online and in print; yet, we have never found a proper Bible study resource that quite met our needs. This is what inspired me to consider writing such a book, and when a new study opportunity arose, I prayerfully endeavored to begin researching and drafting. So, this book is a reflection of what I perceive to be a healthy balance of biblical insight and interactive reflection. Whether you are being discipled or are discipling others, I pray you would benefit from this study of God's word.

This guide divides the book of Galatians into fourteen sections. Each section begins with a series of connection questions, allowing the reader to establish a relationship with one of the passage's themes. If you are working in a one-on-one, small group or large Bible study setting, then you may use these connection questions as a starting point for your discussion.

Next, you will find two to three pages of Background and Context. These sections will include cross-references, summaries of previous chapters and explanations to help you read between the lines. Following this contextualization comes the passage itself. I encourage you to highlight and mark it up however you desire.

INTRODUCTION

    Then, you will encounter a few pages of Insights and Exposition. This is the commentary section of this guide, providing you with key information that will help you interpret the text accurately. Moving from this interpretation, you will be prompted with questions pertaining to the passage's key concepts. These questions will check your understanding of the passage and help you apply it to your theological worldview.

    Lastly, each chapter concludes with an Application. Studying the Bible is not merely so your mind can be full, but that through your mind the Scripture may permeate your heart. This section helps accomplish just that.

KEY INFORMATION ON GALATIANS

AUTHOR

The Apostle Paul is the author of Galatians. A former Pharisee and legalistic zealot, Paul encountered Christ on the road to Damascus, an experience that God used to transform him from a persecutor of the church to an apostle of it (Acts 9:1-19; Phil. 3:2-11).

In Galatians 1:1, he establishes himself as the writer of the epistle and does so again in 5:2. He writes much of the letter in an autobiographical manner, confirming his apostolic status and right to proclaim the gospel of Christ.

Throughout the world of biblical scholarship, Galatians is one of the New Testament letters that are undisputedly Pauline. Few scholars have posited that it was a forgery written at a later point in time—1 and 2 Corinthians are also widely regarded as Pauline. The works of the Apostle Peter and many early church fathers contain quotations or allusions to Galatians in their works, further marking the letter's position in the biblical canon. Among these fathers were Clement of Alexandria, Polycarp, Justin Martyr, Origen and Irenaeus, to name a few.

INTRODUCTION

OCCASION

False teachers had made their way into the churches of Galatia claiming they were sent from James and the Jerusalem church. Their gospel was twisted. It asserted that salvation was not received by faith alone but through a combination of faith and the Law, particularly the entry rite of circumcision. Prompted by the Galatians' embrace of false teaching, Paul wrote this letter to combat the idea that one must first become a Jew to be justified in God's sight.

Galatians may very well be Paul's earliest, canonical letter. The location of the letter's recipients has an effect on the precision of our dating; we will discuss this in the next section. We can assume that Paul penned this letter with his own hand following the Jerusalem Council as described by Luke in Acts 15. The council met circa A.D. 48. This theory makes sense given Paul's description of his conflict with Peter in 2:11-14 (see chapter 5 of this guide).

INTRODUCTION

AUDIENCE

The Galatians descended from a tribal group known as the Celts. Considered barbarians among Greeks and Romans, this group was conquered by the king of Pergamum, Attalus I in 230 B.C. This ruler confined the group to a small territory near modern-day Turkey. Following their confinement, they were later conquered by the Romans in 189 B.C. The Romans then created a province known as Galatia in 25 B.C., named after the Celtic descendants who lived there, Gallo-Graecians. This province did not include much of the northern region, which can be considered ethnic Galatia. The southern region contained the Roman district of Lycaonia and cities such as Iconium, Derbe and Lystra, which Paul visited on his first journey (Acts 13:14, 14:1-23). This region was not majorly composed of ethnic Galatians as the north was. Paul seems to have traveled to the border of the north, however, in Acts 16 and 18.

Regardless of the exact location of its recipients, the epistle to the Galatians was indeed written to the churches in Galatia; however, we cannot be absolutely sure what region Paul was writing to. If he was writing to the churches of the north, then that places the epistle's date of writing earlier. If he was writing to the churches of the south following a later missionary journey, then that places the date later. Nevertheless, the point of the book still stands: salvation is by grace through faith in Christ.

CHAPTER 1:

A GREETING

GALATIANS 1:1-5

SPARK A CONNECTION

1. Has anyone ever questioned your ability or authority?

_____

_____

_____

_____

2. If so, how did that experience make you feel?

_____

_____

_____

_____

3. Discuss: If you are in a group, share your answers to the previous questions with the person sitting next to you. Be sure to take notes on each other's thoughts.

_____

_____

_____

_____

CHAPTER 1: A GREETING | *Galatians 1:1-5*

BACKGROUND AND CONTEXT

At the beginning of Galatians, Paul comes out swinging. He opens with a refutation of false claims concerning his apostleship and soon after announces a curse upon false teachers. This opening salutation is unlike those of Paul's other canonical epistles, not only because of its rugged tone but because it contains absolutely no commendation or acknowledgment of sainthood. In contrast are the opening verses of Philippians, in which Paul states,

> *To all the saints in Christ Jesus who are at Philippi, with the overseers and deacons ... I thank my God in all my remembrance of you, always in every prayer of mine for you all making my prayer with joy, because of your partnership in the gospel from the first day until now. And I am sure of this, that he who began a good work in you will bring it to completion at the day of Jesus Christ. It is right for me to feel this way about you all, because I hold you in my heart, for you are all partakers with me of grace, both in my imprisonment and in the defense and confirmation of the gospel.*
>
> *- Philippians 1:1b, 3-7*

The absence of such a commendation sets the mood for Galatians' first two chapters. Paul will be defensive of his ministry, reserving any offensive attacks for the wolves that have neutralized the faith of his sheep. These wolves were preaching a gospel that stated one is saved through a combination of faith in Christ and works of the law—specifically the act of circumcision, which was required of all Jewish males. Paul negates this notion and embarks on a mission to bring the Galatian believers back to the right knowledge of the truth.

As you make your way through this short, yet powerful letter, bear in mind the weight of a true gospel presentation. If we preach a gospel that has a slight alteration, then we preach no gospel at all.

We will begin our journey by looking at 1:1-5, Paul's first line of defense against lies and false gospels.

CHAPTER 1: A GREETING | *Galatians 1:1-5*

PASSAGE

GALATIANS 1:1-5

¹ Paul, an apostle—not from men nor through man, but through Jesus Christ and God the Father, who raised him from the dead— ² and all the brothers who are with me,

To the churches of Galatia:

³ Grace to you and peace from God our Father and the Lord Jesus Christ, ⁴ who gave himself for our sins to deliver us from the present evil age, according to the will of our God and Father, ⁵ to whom be the glory forever and ever. Amen.

INSIGHTS AND EXPOSITION

v. 1

"Paul"

> A former Pharisee turned Christ-follower (Acts 9:1-19). Studied under Gamaliel, one of the foremost Second Temple Jewish rabbis (Acts 22:3). Called himself a "Hebrew of Hebrews" (Phil. 3:5).

"Apostle"

> Gr.: *apostolos*, generally, a messenger or emissary. In the context of the church, an apostle was a special emissary of Christ who had seen him in resurrected form and was personally trained by him. Performed wonders and miracles (2 Cor. 12:12). As a group, served as the foundation of the church alongside the prophets (Eph. 2:20).

"who raised him from the dead"

> This proclamation displays how central the gospel is to Paul's mission (Rom. 10:9).

CHAPTER 1: A GREETING | *Galatians 1:1-5*

v. 2

"brothers who are with me"
> This phrase is speaking of those who accompanied Paul on his missionary journey through the region. Perhaps Timothy, Silas and Luke (cf. Acts 16).

vv. 3-5

"Grace to you and peace"
> A common Pauline greeting.

"present evil age"
> This age is marked by evil. Satan is permitted power (2 Cor. 4:4), but we have been delivered from that power (Col. 1:13).

"to whom be the glory forever and ever. Amen."
> See Ps. 72:19; Rom. 11:36; Phil. 4:20; 1 Tim. 1:17.

KEY CONCEPTS

APOSTLESHIP

4. What are the marks of a true apostle?

_____

_____

_____

_____

5. If you were Paul, how would you bolster an argument for your apostleship?

_____

_____

_____

_____

CHAPTER 1: A GREETING | *Galatians 1:1-5*

GETTING THE GOSPEL RIGHT

6. How does Paul explain the gospel in this opening passage?

_____

_____

_____

_____

7. Paul concludes this salutation by speaking of God's glory. Why is this an important point to make at such an early point of his letter? (For reference, read Isaiah 48:9-11.)

_____

_____

_____

_____

APPLICATION

Paul is an apostle of Christ that was set apart for that role from his mother's womb. Though he once persecuted the church, God ordained that he would become a new creation. Just like the Apostle Paul, you have been set apart by God unto new life in him.

Spend some time reading Ephesians 1-2. Consider the myriad riches that have been granted you by our Father in heaven—not because of anything you have done, but solely through grace. After reading this passage, offer a prayer of thanksgiving to the Lord, knowing that despite all of your past sins, wretchedness and depravity, he has chosen you to be made new in Christ (2 Cor. 5:17).

CHAPTER 1: A GREETING | *Galatians 1:1-5*

NOTES

CHAPTER 2:

CURSES

GALATIANS 1:6-10

SPARK A CONNECTION

1. Think of a moment in which you found yourself utterly astonished. Perhaps it was when you found a hair in your meal; or, that time you unintentionally knocked your friend out while playing Twister! Whatever it is, funny or serious, jot it down.

_____
_____
_____
_____

2. Did you feel frustrated? Amused? Bitter? Embarrassed? Describe your emotions at that moment, then share them with the group.

_____
_____
_____
_____

CHAPTER 2: CURSES | *Galatians 1:6-10*

BACKGROUND AND CONTEXT

As we described in the last chapter, Paul is dealing with false teaching in the church. Attacking his God-given authority and the gospel he preaches is a group of ministers who claim to be from the Jerusalem church. Their main assertions are that they are the ones with the true power and the true gospel. They desire to "distort the gospel of Christ" and take believers "into slavery" (1:7; 2:4). Paul is astonished that the Galatian believers are turning away from the true gospel to a corrupt alternative, all at the hands of these liars.

This is not the only location in the New Testament where such a warning and refutation of false teachers is present. In other texts, we see the Scriptural authors prompted to similarly write under the inspiration of the Holy Spirit (2 Tim. 3:16-17; 2 Pt. 1:21). Such an occasion is 2 John 7, "For many deceivers have gone out into the world, those who do not confess the coming of Jesus Christ in the flesh. Such a one is a deceiver and the antichrist." John also writes in his first epistle that we are to "test the spirits to see whether they are from God, for many false prophets have gone out into the world" (1 Jn. 4:1).

During his earthly ministry, our Lord warned his disciples of such false prophets. "Beware of false prophets, who come to you in sheep's clothing but inwardly are ravenous wolves," he told them. "You will recognize them by their fruits" (Matt. 7:15-16). From this premise, Christ goes on to teach about those who will cry out "Lord, Lord!" yet will not be received by him. He does not know these workers of lawlessness (Matt. 7:21-23). Therefore, the proprietors of all false gospels are numbered among such sinful prophets, marked out for destruction because of their corruption and vile debasement.

Through the works of such wicked teachers, the Galatians have been persuaded to turn away. What is so amazing about this turning away is that they have turned their backs on Christ. This is not a refusal of some impersonal or abstract idea, but their Savior himself! Later in the letter, Paul is going to ask a fiery but necessary question: "O foolish Galatians! Who has bewitched you?" (3:1).

As you approach this passage, ask yourself, "Have I ever deserted Christ for something false?"

PASSAGE

GALATIANS 1:6-10

⁶ I am astonished that you are so quickly deserting him who called you in the grace of Christ and are turning to a different gospel— ⁷ not that there is another one, but there are some who trouble you and want to distort the gospel of Christ. ⁸ But even if we or an angel from heaven should preach to you a gospel contrary to the one we preached to you, let him be accursed. ⁹ As we have said before, so now I say again: If anyone is preaching to you a gospel contrary to the one you received, let him be accursed. ¹⁰ For am I now seeking the approval of man, or of God? Or am I trying to please man? If I were still trying to please man, I would not be a servant of Christ.

INSIGHTS AND EXPOSITION

v. 6

"astonished"

> Gr.: *thaumazō*, to marvel or wonder (cf. Rev. 17:6).

"deserting him who called you in the grace of Christ"

> Here, Paul is speaking of the Father, for it is he who calls us by grace into communion with his beloved son (Gal. 1:15; Gal. 5:8). Also, notice that Paul is not stating he is astonished these believers have fallen away after he spent so much time teaching them. His sense of awe is not rooted in his own fleshly efforts, though they are truly apostolic in nature. On the contrary, his awe is rooted in the fact that it is the Lord whom the Galatians are rejecting.

v. 7

"not that there is another one"

> It is clear that there is only one true Gospel, salvation by grace through faith in Christ (Eph. 2:8).

vv. 8-9

"if we or an angel from heaven"

>Paul uses an argument *a fortiori*—lesser to the greater (cf. 1 Cor. 13:1). The purpose of this rhetorical scheme is to emphasize that no messenger can validate a Law-based version of the gospel. If anything is added to faith in Christ, then that gospel is false—period.

"let him be accursed"

>Gr.: *anathema*, cursed. This word specifically refers to damnation.

"As we have said before"

>By repeating this damning statement twice, Paul is emphasizing the just consequence that teachers of such a blatantly erroneous gospel will receive.

v. 10

"For am I now seeking the approval of man, or of God?"
>Paul's primary ministry is to the Lord. He does not need man's approval, but solely that of God. The same applies to his offering of satisfaction and appeasement (v. 10b).

"I would not be a servant of Christ"
>Paul uses the word doulos here, which is translated as "servant." However, it is likely better translated as "slave." The word appears 126 times throughout the New Testament (Matt. 8:9; 10:24-25; 13:27; Rom. 6:16-17).

CHAPTER 2: CURSES | *Galatians 1:6-10*

KEY CONCEPTS

THE GOSPEL

3. What made this gospel false? (v. 6)

_____

_____

_____

_____

4. Are there any religious groups you can identify that teach a different gospel?

_____

_____

_____

_____

POOR TEACHING

5. Pastor John Piper once remarked, "Doctrinal precision and rigor is no luxury. It is a necessity for long-term church health." Do you agree? Why, or why not?

_____

_____

_____

_____

6. How do you reconcile Paul calling out false teachers and Christ's teaching of not judging others? (Matt. 7:1-5)

_____

_____

_____

_____

CHAPTER 2: CURSES | *Galatians 1:6-10*

7. Are there any areas of your life in which you find yourself trying to please others rather than God?

_____

_____

_____

_____

APPLICATION

As followers of Christ, we must remain on guard for the wolves in sheep's clothing. Be sure to abide in the Word. Through it, we arm ourselves against the tactics of the enemy, one of which is false doctrine (Eph. 6:10-20). By submitting to the authority of our elders, we are once again guarded against these attacks (Acts 20:28-30; 1 Tim. 5:20). And lastly, by continually attending the gathering of the saints, we arm ourselves with a third line of defense—a multiplicity of believers who can hold us accountable, pray with us and rejoice over us (Heb. 10:25; Gal. 6:2; 1 Cor. 12:26).

If you have yet to become a member of a local church, ask the Lord to guide you to one so that you may be protected by all three of these defenses. If you have already planted yourself in a local body of believers, then pray about who you may take under your wing. The Lord may very well be calling you to be less of a spectator and more of a disciple-maker.

NOTES

CHAPTER 3:

THE FORMER MURDERER

GALATIANS 1:11-24

SPARK A CONNECTION

1. Have you ever had to prove that you were telling the truth? Or, defend your integrity amidst an assault on your character? Write about that experience.

_____
_____
_____
_____

2. Think of your life before you were saved by Christ. What kind of person were you? Now contrast that person with who you are today. What differences do you see in your attitude, language, values, habits and more?

_____
_____
_____
_____

3. Discuss: Compare your answers with those around you.

CHAPTER 3: THE FORMER MURDERER | *Galatians 1:11-24*

BACKGROUND AND CONTEXT

It is no wonder why the Galatian believers were swiftly deceived when it came to Paul's apostolic status. The man killed Christians! Since he was known as a vicious persecutor of the church, these false teachers were undoubtedly touting Paul's former life in Judaism as a way to deprecate his calling (Acts 22:4; Phil. 3:6). For this reason, when he first attempted to join the believers in Jerusalem, their response was one of fear:

And when he had come to Jerusalem, he attempted to join the disciples. And they were all afraid of him, for they did not believe that he was a disciple.

- Acts 9:26

Coupled with this ad hominem attack against Paul was an attack on his message. If you can silence the messenger, then silencing the message should be a piece of cake. In the passage to come, Paul will defend the gospel he proclaims by stating that he did not receive it from man, but through a revelation of Jesus Christ. As we have discussed before, one of the qualifications of an apostle was to see the risen Christ. You also had to be taught by him.

This is why Paul will be devoting this next pericope (section of Scripture) to a historical description of his conversion experience. If he does not quell the questions of his origins at the outset of the letter, then much of what he will say later on will be rendered null and void.

In the book of Acts, we read Luke's description of Paul's conversion experience while on his way to persecute the church:

> *Now as he went on his way, he approached Damascus, and suddenly a light from heaven shone around him. And falling to the ground, he heard a voice saying to him, "Saul, Saul, why are you persecuting me?" And he said, "Who are you, Lord?" And he said, "I am Jesus, whom you are persecuting. But rise and enter the city, and you will be told what you are to do." The men who were traveling with him stood speechless, hearing the voice but seeing no one. Saul rose from the ground, and although his eyes were opened, he saw nothing. So they led him by the hand and brought him into Damascus. And for three days he was without sight, and neither ate nor drank.*
>
> - Acts 9:3-9

After having this remarkable experience with the risen Jesus, Paul is trained by the Spirit of God for three years. He did not immediately consult flesh and blood, according to Galatians 1:16, nor did he join any of the apostles so as to be taught by them (1:17). This is all to say that Paul received his message directly from the Lord himself. The Galatians needed to know this very message was the pure, unadulterated truth.

PASSAGE

GALATIANS 1:11-24

[11] For I would have you know, brothers, that the gospel that was preached by me is not man's gospel. [12] For I did not receive it from any man, nor was I taught it, but I received it through a revelation of Jesus Christ. [13] For you have heard of my former life in Judaism, how I persecuted the church of God violently and tried to destroy it. [14] And I was advancing in Judaism beyond many of my own age among my people, so extremely zealous was I for the traditions of my fathers. [15] But when he who had set me apart before I was born, and who called me by his grace, [16] was pleased to reveal his Son to me, in order that I might preach him among the Gentiles, I did not immediately consult with anyone; [17] nor did I go up to Jerusalem to those who were apostles before me, but I went away into Arabia, and returned again to Damascus.

[18] Then after three years I went up to Jerusalem to visit Cephas and remained with him fifteen days. [19] But I saw none of the other apostles except James the Lord's brother. [20] (In what I am writing to you, before God, I do not lie!) [21] Then I went into the regions of Syria and Cilicia. [22] And I was still unknown in person to the churches of Judea that are in Christ. [23] They only were hearing it said, "He who used to persecute us is now preaching the faith he once tried to destroy." [24] And they glorified God because of me.

INSIGHTS AND EXPOSITION
vv. 11-12

"For I would have you know"
> Gr.: *gnorizō gar hymin*. *Gnorizō* means to make clear. Paul wants his readers to know very well that his gospel was not made up by human imagination, or according to humanity (Gr.: *kata anthrōpon*).

"receive it from man"
> In combination, the preposition para and the verb paralambanō specifically denote the transmission of religious instruction.

"but I received it through a revelation of Jesus Christ"
> See Background and Context.

CHAPTER 3: THE FORMER MURDERER | *Galatians 1:11-24*

vv. 13-14

"For you have heard of my former life in Judaism"
> Paul was a zealous follower of Judaism. See ch. 1, Insights and Exposition.

"so extremely zealous was I"
> See Phil. 3:4-6

vv. 15-16

"set me apart before I was born"
> Can also be translated as, "set me apart from my mother's womb" (cf. Jer. 1:5; Ps. 139:13).

"who called me by his grace"
> Salvation is conferred by God's grace.

"that I might preach him among the Gentiles"
> Paul was the apostle to the Gentiles, while Peter was the apostle to the Jews (Gal. 2:7-8).

v. 17

>Paul did not meet with the apostles after his salvation. Rather, he went away into Arabia.

vv. 18-20

"Then after three years"
>After a three-year period, Paul finally consults with other apostles, James and Peter.

"In what I am writing to you, before God, I do not lie!"
>Once again, Paul wants to make sure that his honesty is directly communicated.

CHAPTER 3: THE FORMER MURDERER | *Galatians 1:11-24*

vv. 21-24

"I went into the regions of Syria and Cilicia"
> Paul was from Cilicia. His hometown of Tarsus was located here (Acts 11:25).

"I was still unknown"
> Paul remained relatively quiet during these years. It would be long before he gained the notoriety we know him for today.

"They were only hearing it said"
> Since Paul lived in obscurity, word had spread concerning his conversion. For this reason, the church praised God all the more: "And they glorified God because of me" (v. 24).

KEY CONCEPTS

PROVIDENTIAL GRACE

4. In verse 15, Paul states that the Lord set him apart before he was born. Read Romans 8:28-30. What does being set apart look like?

CHAPTER 3: THE FORMER MURDERER | *Galatians 1:11-24*

5. Paul was called by grace. What exactly is God's grace? How should we define it? Write down a moment in Scripture in which you see the grace of God directly applied.

_____
_____
_____
_____

6. Name a few areas of your life where God's grace is transparently evident.

_____
_____
_____
_____

APPLICATION

It is far too easy for us to look at someone's past and downplay their future. The Galatians had believed a lie concerning the Apostle Paul partially because they had a difficult time understanding how God could save such a wretched man. Still, it pleased God to save this wretch, and it pleased him to save a wretch like you (1:16). God redeemed you from a life of sin. He snatched you from the course of this world in which you once walked (Eph. 2:1-4).

Before we move into Galatians 2, take a moment to reflect on the themes of Galatians 1. Then, read these few stanzas from the classic hymn, "Amazing Grace."

> *Amazing Grace how sweet the sound,*
> *That saved a wretch like me!*
> *I once was lost, but now am found;*
> *Was blind, but now I see.*
> *'Twas grace that taught my heart to fear,*
> *And grace my fears relieved;*
> *How precious did that grace appear*
> *The hour I first believed!*
> *Through many dangers, toils, and snares,*
> *I have already come;*
> *'Tis grace hath brought me safe thus far,*
> *And grace will lead me home.*
>
> *- John Newton, "Amazing Grace," 1779*

CHAPTER 3: THE FORMER MURDERER | *Galatians 1:11-24*

NOTES

CHAPTER 4:

PAUL IS ACCEPTED

GALATIANS 2:1-10

SPARK A CONNECTION

1. Has anyone of influence ever commended you for service? Perhaps your boss thanked you for always arriving to work a few minutes earlier than expected. Maybe your pastor acknowledged you for always being the first to clean up a mess, even when it isn't your job. Write about such an experience.

2. As Christians, we must be ready to serve those around us. Do you see yourself as a self-giving person, always seeking to help the poor, pray for the hopeless or offer assistance to those in need?

3. Discuss: How can you as an individual, and those around you as a collective group, improve in generosity and service?

CHAPTER 4: PAUL IS ACCEPTED | *Galatians 2:1-10*

BACKGROUND AND CONTEXT

You are in the midst of a rather long, autobiographical exposition of Paul's life. So, if chapter three of this guide felt like a lot to take in, know that we will soon be arriving at the more glorious sections of this epistle. Nevertheless, do not gloss over any word of the letter itself. Digest all that Galatians has to offer, even seeking illumination from its most "dry" sections (after all, these sections are still the word of the living God).

New Testament scholars debate the point where Paul's personal, rhetorical stage of Galatians ends. We know that it begins at 1:11 since Paul signifies a transition between curses on false teachers and his apostolic experience in 1:10; however, it could end at 2:10 or 2:21. There is not much of a need to dive into this discussion given the scope of this guide, but if you desire to nerd out over the specifics, check out Douglas Moo's chapter, "The Truth of the Gospel (1:11-2:21)" in the Baker Exegetical Commentary series. You can find the reference information at the back of this book.

In 1:11-1:24, Paul is describing his apostleship from a vertical perspective—from God on high to him down below. This is necessary given the nature of the apostolic calling and the prerequisites an apostle needed to meet. Now, in 2:1 - 2:14, Paul will be describing his apostleship horizontally—from him to the other apostles, both of whom are here below.

This framing is necessary to understand Paul's task. As the biblical scholar, D.A. Carson, once remarked, "A text without a context is a pretext for a prooftext." That's a lot of scholarly jargon, so in layman's terms, "If you use a portion of Scripture without understanding the information within, above and beneath it, then you will abuse it." We don't want to be abusers of the text, now do we? So, getting accurate information concerning our text's background (or any text for that matter) is vital, lest those of us who labor in preaching and teaching find ourselves as workers who need to be ashamed (2 Tim. 2:15).

In this new stage of Paul's rhetorical scheme, what I call the horizontal stage, Paul will be writing on his second meeting with other apostles, most prominently Peter. The first is seen in 1:18, the second in 2:1 for the Jerusalem council on circumcision (Acts 15) and the third in 2:11, which we will discuss in the next chapter.

Paul is now detailing his acceptance by the apostles. The ministry he has performed alongside other servants such as Barnabas and Titus is officially recognized by the church. James, Peter and John offer Paul and his companions "the right hand of fellowship," verifying their ministry to the uncircumsized just as they have verified Peter's to the circumsized (2:9). They merely requested that they remember the poor in all that they do, a duty that was already on Paul's heart.

CHAPTER 4: PAUL IS ACCEPTED | *Galatians 2:1-10*

PASSAGE

GALATIANS 2:1-10

¹ Then after fourteen years I went up again to Jerusalem with Barnabas, taking Titus along with me. ² I went up because of a revelation and set before them (though privately before those who seemed influential) the gospel that I proclaim among the Gentiles, in order to make sure I was not running or had not run in vain. ³ But even Titus, who was with me, was not forced to be circumcised, though he was a Greek. ⁴ Yet because of false brothers secretly brought in—who slipped in to spy out our freedom that we have in Christ Jesus, so that they might bring us into slavery— ⁵ to them we did not yield in submission even for a moment, so that the truth of the gospel might be preserved for you. ⁶ And from those who seemed to be influential (what they were makes no difference to me; God shows no partiality)—those, I say, who seemed influential added nothing to me. ⁷ On the contrary, when they saw that I had been entrusted with the gospel to the uncircumcised, just as Peter had been entrusted with the gospel to the circumcised ⁸ (for he who worked through Peter for his apostolic ministry to the circumcised worked also through me for mine to the Gentiles), ⁹ and when James and Cephas and John, who seemed to be pillars, perceived the grace that was given to me, they gave the right hand of fellowship to Barnabas and me, that we should go to the Gentiles and they to the circumcised. ¹⁰ Only, they asked us to remember the poor, the very thing I was eager to do.

INSIGHTS AND EXPOSITION

vv. 1-2

"Then after fourteen years"
> Paul seems to be stating that this period of fourteen years marks the time that had passed from his last visit with the apostles. His first meeting likely occurred circa A.D. 35. His second meeting—the one he is now speaking of—likely occurred in A.D. 49.

"I went up because of a revelation"
> Paul was drawn to Jerusalem by the will of God, not the will of the apostles (cf. 1:1).

"in order to make sure I was not running ... in vain"
> Interestingly enough, Paul needed confirmation that the churches he had planted through the gospel were legitimate.

CHAPTER 4: PAUL IS ACCEPTED | *Galatians 2:1-10*

vv. 3-5

"But even Titus ... though he was a Greek"
> Titus' Gentile status would compel the Judaizers to try to impose circumcision upon him.

"to them we did not yield in submission"
> Paul is speaking of his triumph over these legalists for the preservation of the truth.

v. 6

"those ... who seemed influential added nothing to me"
> Paul is reiterating the notion that the apostles did not lend themselves to his authority. It was solely of God.

vv. 7-10

"the gospel to the uncircumcised"

> The King James Version translates this phrase as "the gospel of the uncircumcised," thus suggesting to the reader that there are two different gospels: Paul's and Peter's. This, however, is not an accurate or true rendering of the original text. We must know that there is simply one gospel.

"James and Cephas and John"

> The apostles are equal in influence, yet differ in sphere. James is mentioned first since he is the leader of the Jerusalem council.

"Only, they asked us to remember the poor, the very thing I was eager to do"

> cf. Acts 11:27-30. Paul had a deep concern for the poor and the generosity of Christians (Rom. 15:26; 2 Cor. 9:6-8).

CHAPTER 4: PAUL IS ACCEPTED | *Galatians 2:1-10*

KEY CONCEPTS

PAUL'S CALL AND GOSPEL

4. Why was it necessary for Paul to consistently affirm that he was called by God? (2:2).

_____

_____

_____

_____

5. In verse 4, Paul writes of "false brothers secretly brought in." How can we protect the true brethren in light of Satan's scheme to sow tares among the wheat?

_____

_____

_____

_____

6. The writer of "Amazing Grace," John Newton, once said, "The best method of defeating heresy is by establishing the truth. One proposes to fill a bushel with tares; now if I can fill it with wheat, I shall defeat his attempts." William Plummer, a 19th century clergymen, disagreed. He dissented in stating, "Surely the truth ought to be abundantly set forth. But this is not sufficient. The human mind is not like a bushel. It may learn much truth and yet go after folly." Quoting 2 Timothy 4:2, Plummer exhorted pastors to "preach the word," "rebuke" heretical beliefs, and "exhort with complete patience and teaching." Which perspective do you think is more effective: Newton's passivity or Plummer's activity? Why?

_____

_____

_____

_____

_____

CHAPTER 4: PAUL IS ACCEPTED | *Galatians 2:1-10*

GENEROSITY

7. Paul writes that he was eager to help the poor (2:10). Likewise, we understand that giving is a requirement for citizens of God's kingdom. For Israel, the Law required that they give their tithe to the Lord. For Christians, the Law has been fulfilled by Christ (Matt. 5:17). Yet, simply because we are under a different covenant does not dispense us of withholding finances from the Lord. Read 1 Corinthians 16:2 and 2 Corinthians 9:6-7. Are you a cheerful and generous giver? What does giving "as [you] may prosper" look like?

_____

_____

_____

_____

_____

_____

APPLICATION

As a Christian, you need to stand firm on God's truth. If you are wavering when it comes to your understanding of the gospel, take some time to reflect on what you need confirmed or denied. If you are fearing that your work has been in vain, just as Paul did, search for the reason why. Be sure to discuss these matters with the Lord in prayer and with fellow believers whom you trust.

Also, if you have been withholding your finances from God and his church, know that you are not walking in step with the Lord's will for your life. Far too many Christians give to the Lord after the fact. "I'll give my offering after I pay my bills," they say in their minds. However, this is not the thought-life we should maintain. Instead, we should tell ourselves, "I'll pay my bills after I give what belongs to the Lord."

God should not get your scraps. Offer him your first fruits and he will provide for you. If you are in dire need of extra assurance when it comes to this matter, prayerfully examine Matthew 6:24-34.

NOTES

CHAPTER 5:

FACING HYPOCRISY

GALATIANS 2:11–14

SPARK A CONNECTION

1. Think of a time when you experienced disappointment in someone you personally admire or care for. What did they do that caused you to think differently of them?

_____

_____

_____

_____

2. Did you express your disappointment to them in hopes of resolving the issue? What was that experience like?

_____

_____

_____

_____

3. Discuss: If you are comfortable, share your disappointment with the group and the way you went about resolving the issue? Or, if you did not resolve it, explain why.

CHAPTER 5: FACING HYPOCRICY | *Galatians 2:11-14*

BACKGROUND AND CONTEXT

In the previous chapter, we observed how Paul established his unity with the apostles. After discussing his vertical relationship with God, he discusses his horizontal relationship with the men whom Christ ordained as his very own ambassadors. Mixed in with Paul's argument were two occasions in which he met with some of his fellow apostles. Here, in 2:11-14, we read of his third meeting: a confrontation.

As we now know, Peter was the apostle to the Jews. He may very well have been a superstar among them. The man walked on water, preached to thousands and would go on to write two books of the New Testament, also serving as the main contributor to Mark's gospel. Even today, members of the Roman Catholic church regard their pope as speaking ex-cathedra, implying infallible speech on the grounds of apostolic succession. Regardless of the many issues with this assertion, in this, they mean that given the continuation of the apostolic gift, the pope bears the same authority Peter exercised when he wrote his epistles. As I digress, Peter was and still is a big guy.

Yet, he was just a man. Before Christ, he was a common fisherman, and after Christ, he returned to that same vocation (John 21:1-4). He was the first among the disciples to acknowledge who Jesus really was; however, he was also the only one who would deny him three times (Matt. 16:13-20; 26:69-75).

This goes to show that God can use sinful people to produce righteous things. While Peter was just like you and me, God still used him to write his words so that those in the ages to come may have a knowledge of the truth.

In our next passage, Paul will be confronting Peter, declaring him a hypocrite. No mere Christian would dare go toe-to-toe with an inspired apostle, but Paul did. He was able to do so because of his own apostolic authority, further proving his status as one of Christ's emissaries and foundations of the church.

Paul is expressing frustration over Peter's capitulation to teachers who claim to be from the Apostle James in Jerusalem. It is likely that James did not send these men. Instead, they had likely lied about their origins. Because Peter did not stand up to these wolves as Paul had when they confronted both him and Titus, Paul has an axe to grind with him. Additionally, many Christians were following Peter in his malpractice to the extent that Barnabas, Paul's missionary companion, had followed suit.

Ironically, Peter had previously seen a vision in which God told him that all food was now clean:

CHAPTER 5: FACING HYPOCRICY | *Galatians 2:11-14*

The next day, as they were on their journey and approaching the city, Peter went up on the housetop about the sixth hour to pray. And he became hungry and wanted something to eat, but while they were preparing it, he fell into a trance and saw the heavens opened and something like a great sheet descending, being let down by its four corners upon the earth. In it were all kinds of animals and reptiles and birds of the air. And there came a voice to him: "Rise, Peter; kill and eat." But Peter said, "By no means, Lord; for I have never eaten anything that is common or unclean." And the voice came to him again a second time, "What God has made clean, do not call common." This happened three times, and the thing was taken up at once to heaven.

- *Acts 9:10-16*

Despite having this revelation, Peter does not stand his ground when it comes to eating with Gentiles, reinforcing the Jewish notion that Gentiles were unclean and separated from God. Paul confronts this lie with equal amounts of force and precision and will drive this point home at other points in the letter (See 3:28-29).

PASSAGE

GALATIANS 2:11-14

[11] But when Cephas came to Antioch, I opposed him to his face, because he stood condemned. [12] For before certain men came from James, he was eating with the Gentiles; but when they came he drew back and separated himself, fearing the circumcision party. [13] And the rest of the Jews acted hypocritically along with him, so that even Barnabas was led astray by their hypocrisy. [14] But when I saw that their conduct was not in step with the truth of the gospel, I said to Cephas before them all, "If you, though a Jew, live like a Gentile and not like a Jew, how can you force the Gentiles to live like Jews?"

CHAPTER 5: FACING HYPOCRICY | *Galatians 2:11-14*

INSIGHTS AND EXPOSITION

v. 11

"Cephas"
> The Aramaic name for Peter.

"I opposed him face to face"
> Yet another example of Paul's apostolic authority. He was public with his criticism against Peter.

"he stood condemned"
> In this sense, Peter did not somehow lose his status as an apostle; nor did he somehow lose his salvation. Instead, he stood as a guilty sinner in the face of Paul and the Gentile believers he dismissed. He appeared to be affirming the breach of the Judaizers publicly; therefore, Paul opposed him publicly. This is a church practice that has gone out of vogue (Matt. 18:15-17). Additionally, Paul was not committed to artificial unity like Peter was. He desired harmony founded solely on the truth of the gospel and was willing to risk his reputation for the recovery of that form of unity.

v. 12

"he was eating with the Gentiles"

>Here, the imperfect tense is used in reference to Peter's eating. This implies that Peter ate with Gentiles habitually, signifying the unity that now exists between Israel and all other people groups.

"but when they came he drew back"

>That active phrase, "drew back," is translated from *hupostellō*, which refers to an army withdrawing from battle for security.

v. 13

"hypocritically"

>From the word, *upokrisis*: lack of sincerity; play-acting.

"so that even Barnabas was led away"
> At the time, Barnabas was an elder at the church in Antioch and had previously assisted Paul as a missionary. He, too, was misled.

v. 14

"their conduct was not in step"
> This phrase comes from the word, *orthopodeō*. Orthos (straight) and pous (foot); to walk straightly or uprightly.

"If you, though a Jew … to live like Jews?"
> Paul's question is straightforward, unlike Peter's example. The intention of the question is not to puff Paul up at the cost of his brother, but to correct the devious error that had now been proliferated throughout the church.

KEY CONCEPTS

CONFRONTING ERROR

4. How should Christians settle conflict or confront error among fellow believers?

___

___

___

___

5. What should a church do with an unrepentant congregant according to Matthew 18:15-17?

___

___

___

___

CHAPTER 5: FACING HYPOCRICY | *Galatians 2:11-14*

6. How would you describe Paul's tone in the letter thus far?

_____

_____

_____

_____

7. Are there areas of your life in which you are living hypocritically?

_____

_____

_____

_____

8. Write down any questions you have about the text to prompt further investigation.

APPLICATION

Peter walked with Jesus. Of all the people on earth, wouldn't we expect him to be the most perfect? Despite the high expectations we may have of him, he was imperfect. The truth is that you and I are just as imperfect as he was; as in need of grace as he was; as volatile as he was; as depraved as he was; as sinful as he was; "but God shows his love for us in that while we were still sinners, Christ died for us" (Rom. 5:8).

There is an inherent beauty to this truth. It is a beatific statement, and one that should ignite the highest doxology and praise within our souls while making room for the deepest, heartiest worship. May you reflect on the Father's love for you demonstrated through Christ's death on the cross. You were supposed to be hung on that tree, but the creator of universe—the very Word of God—came to die in your place on Calvary's hill (Jn. 1:1-5).

How deep the Father's love for us,
How vast beyond all measure,
That He should give His only Son,
To make a wretch his treasure.

How great the pain of searing loss
The Father turns his face away
As wounds which mar the Chosen One
Bring many sons to glory.

Behold the man upon a cross,
My sin upon his shoulders;
Ashamed I hear my mocking voice
Call out among the scoffers.

It was my sin that held Him there.
Until it was accomplished;
His dying breath has brought me life —
I know that it is finished.

I will not boast in anything,
No gifts, no power, no wisdom;
But I will boast in Jesus Christ,
His death and resurrection.

Why should I gain from His reward?
I cannot give an answer;
But this I know with all my heart —
His wounds have paid my ransom.

- Stuart Townend, "How Deep the Father's Love for Us," 1990

NOTES

CHAPTER 6:

JUSTIFICATION BY FAITH

---

*GALATIANS
2:15-21*

SPARK A CONNECTION

1. For a moment, imagine that salvation was dependent on your fulfillment of the Law—all 613 commandments! Would you be able to attain salvation?

_____

_____

_____

_____

2. What holds you back from living a perfect and sinless life? Why do you need to trust in Christ's righteousness instead of your own?

_____

_____

_____

_____

3. Know that Christ has accomplished salvation for you through his perfect faithfulness. He did what you could not. Before moving on to the content of this next passage, meditate on the loving- kindness he has extended to you. Consider reading Deuteronomy 7:9 and John 15:12-13 independently or as a group.

CHAPTER 6: JUSTIFICATION BY FAITH | *Galatians 2:15-21*

BACKGROUND AND CONTEXT

We now arrive at the crux of Galatians. If Paul's letter was a door, then 2:15-21 would be its hinge. Without this crucial section, the letter would be confusing and its argument would nearly fall apart. There is much that could be said about this passage, so as you read about its context and the expository notes to follow, know that there is so much more to be uncovered. Also, don't rush through this passage. Whether you are a trained biblical scholar or a baby Christian, these few verses will never cease to amaze you (though I've read them innumerable times, they have never failed).

There are a few key points that you need to know about this series of verses. First, many scholars contend that 2:15-21 is the thesis of the letter. If you went to high school or college, you were likely assigned papers that required a thesis statement. This was a sentence, or two, that narrowed down the topic you would be writing about, serving as a helpful guide for the reader. Therefore, as stated before, we need such a thesis to understand where Paul is taking his original audience.

Second, Paul's central point is that we are justified by faith, not by works of the Law. "The Epistle to the Galatians is my epistle," Martin Luther once admirably stated, "It is my Katie von Bora" (the name of his wife). Luther was a Roman Catholic monk who was so concerned about his sin that he spent hours in the confessional, leading some church historians to believe he suffered from OCD or anxiety. It was Galatians' doctrine of justification by faith alone, as he and other Reformers would phrase it, that was necessary to release him from his bondage.

Third, and this is a more complex point, we do not really know if Paul is still continuing the recount of his speech from 2:11-14, or if he is now speaking directly to the Galatians. There are a couple of reasons why, and I will do my best to not get over-scholarly (however, if you don't mind digging through academic work, see Yoon in the bibliography).

1) We know that ancient languages such as Koine Greek—the majority language of the New Testament—did not have punctuation marks, making it difficult to discern whether the writer is making an original statement or quoting another person. If you are unaware, another example of this difficulty is found in every Christian's favorite verse, John 3:16. We do not know with certainty that Jesus ever said those words, as John may have been inserting his own editorialization as a conclusion to Jesus' conversation with Nicodemus (I am sorry if that statement somehow shattered your soul or something. It freaked me out when I first heard it as a wee-Bible student. Don't fear, we are not forced to get rid of our John 3:16 coffee mugs and bumper stickers. The verse is still the word of God).

2) To add more complexity to this situation, ancient manuscripts did not have spaces in between words or paragraph indentions and only contained upper case letters (until the fourth century's Codex Sinaiticus, the oldest codex to contain the entire Bible and utilize upper and lower case script—pretty cool). As a professor of mine once put it, you and I gloss over our nicely formatted English Bibles; but, for an ancient Christian to read the Bible like us, they would have to solve an entire puzzle per verse. If I may add to the analogy, the box the puzzle came in contains a pixelated, 8-bit image of what the puzzle should look like in the end. Sure, you can get the general framework, but not the nitty-gritty, so to speak. Imagine that as your daily devotional!

Now that we've got all that out of the way, let's get into the text.

PASSAGE

GALATIANS 2:15-21

¹⁵ We ourselves are Jews by birth and not Gentile sinners; ¹⁶ yet we know that a person is not justified by works of the law but through faith in Jesus Christ, so we also have believed in Christ Jesus, in order to be justified by faith in Christ and not by works of the law, because by works of the law no one will be justified.

¹⁷ But if, in our endeavor to be justified in Christ, we too were found to be sinners, is Christ then a servant of sin? Certainly not! ¹⁸ For if I rebuild what I tore down, I prove myself to be a transgressor. ¹⁹ For through the law I died to the law, so that I might live to God. ²⁰ I have been crucified with Christ. It is no longer I who live, but Christ who lives in me. And the life I now live in the flesh I live by faith in the Son of God, who loved me and gave himself for me. ²¹ I do not nullify the grace of God, for if righteousness were through the law, then Christ died for no purpose.

CHAPTER 6: JUSTIFICATION BY FAITH | *Galatians 2:15-21*

INSIGHTS AND EXPOSITION

v. 15

"We ourselves are Jews by birth"

Whether or not Paul is still quoting himself here, the Antioch incident is still on his mind. He desires his audience to know that being a Jew and following the Law is not enough for one to stand righteous before Holy God (cf. Romans 9:1-5).

v. 16

"a person is not justified by works of the law but through faith in Jesus Christ"

1) This very well may be the most important statement in the entire Bible. We are not made right with God through our own actions of law-keeping. We are made right through faith in Christ. This faith is not the source of our righteousness, but the means of attainment, for Christ is the one who imputes his righteousness unto us (2 Cor. 5:21).

2) The verb, "justify," is *dikaioō*, which is a forensic term used in a court of law. It denotes an act of acquittal or pardoning apart from one's own merit, thus, in the Christian sense,

bringing the formerly guilty into the fold of God's people. This is the first time that the term "justification" in its various forms is used in the epistle. "Law" is also mentioned for the first time in this verse.

"so we also have believed in Christ Jesus"

This insertion in the middle of the verse expounds upon the meaning of faith. Faith and belief are not mere expressions of the cognitive recognition of facts, but heartfelt trust in the truth. Therefore, Christians do not simply believe in Christ, but trust in him.

"because by works of the law no one will be justified"

Here is a use of parallelism, a literary device that unites multiple sentences through similar syntactical and grammatical structures. This is a very popular device in the wisdom literature.

v. 17

"But if"

Paul is now going to be answering possible counterarguments to his previous assertion in v. 16.

"we too were found to be sinners"

> Those of the circumcision party thought that justification by faith alone would lead to an antinomian gospel (anti: against; nomos, law). These legalists did not understand that Christians are not saved by good works, but for them. The gospel of grace does not permit us to live however we like; yet, it provides grace for our stumbles (Rom. 5:20).

vv. 18-19

"For if I rebuild what I tore down, I prove myself to be a transgressor"

> If you come to a knowledge of the truth then turn to your own self-righteousness, you are enabling sin in your life (cf. Heb. 6:4-6).

"For through the law, I died to the law, so that I might live to God"

> This indicates that the Law is a tutor unto Christ. It exposes our sin and unrighteousness, leaving Christ as the only means of true justification. We have died to the Law; therefore, we cannot return to it.

v. 20

"I have been crucified with Christ ... but Christ who lives in me"

> 1) Christians identify themselves with Christ's crucifixion and resurrection. This is a spiritual participation in both events through union with Christ (Col. 2:12-14, 20).
>
> 2) "I have been crucified" is a perfect tense phrase, implying that though the crucifixion happened in the past, its effects still ring in the present.

"And the life I now live in the flesh I live by faith in the Son of God"

> Paul's life has been radically transformed by the experience of faith. He does not live according to his own righteousness, but Christ's.

v. 21

""I do not nullify the grace of God"

> "Nullify" is to invalidate something or cancel it out.

"for if righteousness were through the law, then Christ died for no purpose"

> If our salvation is achieved by carnal efforts to fulfill the law's strict ordinances, then Christ's incarnation, earthly ministry, death and bodily resurrection were meaningless.

KEY CONCEPTS

JUSTIFICATION

4. When you consider God's holiness and your sinfulness, what emotions strike you? Do you become fearful? Anxious? Worried?

_____

5. Given the sin of the world and its rebellion against the Lord, do you believe humanity is deserving of mercy? For biblical examples of such rebellion, read Deuteronomy 12:31 and Psalm 2.

_____

CHAPTER 6: JUSTIFICATION BY FAITH | *Galatians 2:15-21*

6. If someone asked you how they could be made right with God, how would you reply? Detail a brief response here.

_____

_____

_____

_____

7. How should you live knowing that Christ lives in you? (v. 20)

_____

_____

_____

_____

_____

_____

APPLICATION

You cannot live on your own accord. Sadly, some Christians try to. There are far too many gospel presentations that cause the sinner to believe that despite the way they live their lives, they can just pray a prayer and be set for all eternity. This is Satanic and untrue. Antinomianism is just as dangerous as legalism. Neither of these ways are the way of Jesus.

We are justified by faith alone, yet not by a faith that comes alone. Given this truth, how have you demonstrated your position as a child of God? Do you not only believe facts about him, but do you trust in him? Do you only pray before meals, or are you constantly in communication with him? Is your Bible collecting dust on the shelf just waiting for the next hard time to come around, or do you open it routinely throughout the week? These are but a few points to ponder as we conclude this important chapter.

In the next chapter, we will be analyzing Galatians 3:1-9. This is another beefy and important section, so stay tuned. I think you will receive much illumination from it.

CHAPTER 6: JUSTIFICATION BY FAITH | *Galatians 2:15-21*

NOTES

CHAPTER 7:

BEWITCHED

GALATIANS 3:1-9

SPARK A CONNECTION

1. Have you ever been tricked? Perhaps a friend pulled a prank on you, or your local car dealership locked you into a contract that had pesky hidden fees. Detail such a time and how it occurred.

_____

_____

_____

_____

2. Bearing this in mind, have you ever been tricked by false doctrine? Perhaps in your early days as a Christian, or as a member of a denomination with unbiblical practices? How did you fall for these teachings?

_____

_____

_____

_____

3. Discuss: If you are in a group, share the teachings you fell for. Talk about ways you can all protect yourselves against error in the future.

CHAPTER 7: BEWITCHED | *Galatians 3:1-9*

BACKGROUND AND CONTEXT

I am sure you have heard of a man named Abraham. If you grew up in church, you probably had to dance to the Christian hokey-pokey, also known as "Father Abraham." Even if you came to the faith later in life, you may have heard of the three Abrahamic religions: Judaism, Christianity and Islam.

The Jews regarded Abraham as the highest example of faithfulness. In a time before the Mosaic Law existed, Abraham proved himself to be faithful to the Lord and was rendered righteous in his sight. Yet, the way the Jews of the Second-Temple era were seeking righteousness was very different from the way of Abraham (Jn. 8:39-40).

Abram (which was his name prior to his covenant with God) came from a pagan nation, used his wife as a scapegoat to save his own life and had no prior merits to show the Lord. However, in his grace, God called Abram to be the conduit by which he would bless the whole world.

> *Now the Lord said to Abram, "Go from your country and your kindred and your father's house to the land that I will show you. And I will make of you a great nation, and I will bless you and make your name great, so that you will be a blessing. I will bless those who bless you, and him who dishonors you I will curse, and in you all the families of the earth shall be blessed."*
>
> *- Genesis 12:1-3*

After this amazing call, God takes Abram on a bit of a journey, ever revealing his plan and character to him. He soon establishes a covenant with Abram, promising that Abram and his wife Sarai will bear a son in their old age.

> *After these things the word of the Lord came to Abram in a vision: "Fear not, Abram, I am your shield; your reward shall be very great." But Abram said, "O Lord God, what will you give me, for I continue childless, and the heir of my house is Eliezer of Damascus?" And Abram said, "Behold, you have given me no offspring, and a member of my household will be my heir." And behold, the word of the Lord came to him: "This man shall not be your heir; your very own son shall be your heir." And he brought him outside and said, "Look toward heaven, and number the stars, if you are able to number them." Then he said to him, "So shall your offspring be." And he believed the Lord, and he counted it to him as righteousness.*
>
> *- Genesis 15:1-6*

CHAPTER 7: BEWITCHED | *Galatians 3:1-9*

That final verse is the foundational verse of the gospel, and it is not even found in the New Testament, but in the very first book of the Bible! Abraham did nothing but place his faith in God and he was credited righteousness. This was a type and shadow of what Christ would do for you and me, providing a righteousness foreign to us which we could not attain.

In Galatians 3:1-9, Paul will harken back to this amazing moment of the Old Testament, using it as an alarm to snap the Galatians out of their trance. Switching from an argument from personal experience to an argument from Scripture, he teaches that the Galatians are children of Abraham by faith, not works of the Law.

PASSAGE

GALATIANS 3:1-9

¹ *O foolish Galatians! Who has bewitched you? It was before your eyes that Jesus Christ was publicly portrayed as crucified.* ² *Let me ask you only this: Did you receive the Spirit by works of the law or by hearing with faith?* ³ *Are you so foolish? Having begun by the Spirit, are you now being perfected by the flesh?* ⁴ *Did you suffer so many things in vain—if indeed it was in vain?* ⁵ *Does he who supplies the Spirit to you and works miracles among you do so by works of the law, or by hearing with faith—* ⁶ *just as Abraham "believed God, and it was counted to him as righteousness"?*

⁷ *Know then that it is those of faith who are the sons of Abraham.* ⁸ *And the Scripture, foreseeing that God would justify the Gentiles by faith, preached the gospel beforehand to Abraham, saying, "In you shall all the nations be blessed."* ⁹ *So then, those who are of faith are blessed along with Abraham, the man of faith.*

CHAPTER 7: BEWITCHED | *Galatians 3:1-9*

INSIGHTS AND EXPOSITION

v. 1

"foolish"

Foolish is translated from the word, *anoetos*, which refers to the behavior of one who can think for themselves, yet acts irrationally. It is a different term than the one Christ often used for foolishness throughout his teachings, moros, which means one who is intellectually deficient or plays the fool as regards morality (Matt. 5:22; 7:26; Lk. 24:25).

"bewitched"

Gr.: *baskainō*, to charm in a misleading way.

"publicly portrayed as crucified"

The Galatians understood the meaning of the cross and were saved in Christ, but were not running in step with their profession of faith. "Publicly portrayed" comes from the word, *prographō*, which refers to a posting of public notices for others to read. In this way, Paul had posted a graphic notice of Christ for the Galatians to see. They had previously seen it and taken it to heart, which is why he is so astonished at their turning away.

vv. 2-3

"Did you ... with faith?"
> Paul is asking the Galatians a rhetorical question. He knows the answer, but he wants them to say the answer: "We received the Spirit not by works, but by faith." The Spirit is a seal upon the heart of the believer. He indwells all Christians upon salvation (Eph. 1:13-14). The Spirit has set believers free from the law (Rom. 8:1-4).

"Having begun ... the flesh?"
> This question, like the previous one, necessitates a negative response. If one begins in faith, then one must continue in faith.

v. 4

"Did you ... in vain?"
> "Suffer" is translated from *paschō*, which refers to experience in this context rather than labor or hardship.

vv. 5-6

"Does he ... with faith?"

With this statement, Paul has now appealed to the saving power of the entire Trinity. First, he appealed to the Son (v. 1), then the Spirit (v. 2) and now the Father (v. 5). Salvation is accomplished by the Father's election (Jn. 6:44; Rom. 8:29-30; Eph. 1:4-6), the Son's sacrifice (Jn. 3:16; 2 Cor. 5:21) and the Spirit's indwelling (Jn. 14:17).

"Abraham ... 'righteousness'"

Given that Abraham and his descendants were required to be circumcised, it can be rightly inferred that the Judaizers propped up Abraham's circumcision as a reason for Gentile Christians to become circumcised as well (Gen. 17:10). However, Abraham's circumcision came about fourteen years after he was declared righteous in Genesis 15. The Judaizers' logic is clearly flawed.

v. 7

"those who are of faith are sons of Abraham"
> Since Abraham believed, those who do likewise are truly his people (Rom. 4:11-16). We know that not all Israel is Israel. One may consider themselves to be a member of God's people by ethnicity, but that means nothing if they lack faith (Rom. 9:6-8).

v.8

"And the Scripture, foreseeing that God…"
> It has always been God's plan to save the nations through the gospel. The Lord has no plan B, only plan A.

"'In you shall all the nations be blessed'"
> See Background and Context.

"So then … of faith"
> Paul is concluding this portion of the argument. As he is speaking of blessings, he is moving on to the curses contained in the next pericope.

CHAPTER 7: BEWITCHED | *Galatians 3:1-9*

KEY CONCEPTS

GENERAL REVIEW

4. In a sentence or two, how would you summarize this crucial passage?

_____

_____

_____

_____

5. What was so foolish about the Galatians?

_____

_____

_____

_____

THE FAITH OF ABRAHAM

4. Read Hebrews 11:8-12. How does this passage deepen your understanding of faith's power?

_____

_____

_____

_____

5. Abraham was not saved by the ceremonial rite of circumcision, but by faith. Read Romans 2:28-29 and Joel 2:13. What do you see as the difference between outward and inward circumcision? What are their respective outcomes?

_____

_____

_____

_____

APPLICATION

Not too long ago, I overheard a conversation between a Roman Catholic woman and an evangelical man. The newly introduced pair were discussing matters of faith and explaining their religious backgrounds. When the man mentioned he was Protestant, the woman did not seem to mind. "Oh," she casually remarked, "as long as we're good people, then that's all that matters. We're all the same," referring to the different branches of the Christian tradition.

However, this is not true. Our external actions do not matter if our internal posture is not Godly, and the only way to have a Godly internal posture is to be united with Christ by faith alone. The Lord does not "delight in sacrifice," otherwise we would give it. He is not pleased with a "burnt offering." No, the "sacrifices of God are a broken spirit; a broken and contrite heart ... [he] will not despise" (Ps. 51:16-17).

If you have been struggling with maintaining external works, look to the Spirit that dwells within you. He is your guide and your helper, the one who will comfort you in times of trouble. Do not look to yourself for righteousness, "for it is God who works in you, both to will and to work for his good pleasure" (Phil. 2:13).

NOTES

CHAPTER 7: BEWITCHED | *Galatians 3:1-9*

CHAPTER 8:

A CRIMINAL'S DEATH

———

GALATIANS 3:10-18

SPARK A CONNECTION

1. Has someone ever taken the blame for something bad you did? Maybe you broke a vase during your childhood and your sibling said it was their fault. Describe a situation like this in your life.

___

___

___

___

2. What kind of relief did you feel when the circumstance eventually blew over and you no longer had to deal with the anxiety of embarassment or shame?

___

___

___

___

3. Pray: Individually or as a group, thank the Lord for covering the debt of your sin and removing you of all blame. Ask that he may grant you wisdom and insight as you look into the Scriptures for his glory.

CHAPTER 8: A CRIMINAL'S DEATH | *Galatians 3:10-18*

BACKGROUND AND CONTEXT

If you are reading out of the English Standard Version, then you may have noticed that the previous chapters of this guide coincided with the subdivisions present within your ESV Bible. However, for the purpose of this guide, it is necessary to divide chapter 3 a little differently. I'll explain why.

In 3:1-5, Paul is centrally discussing the manner in which believers receive the gift of the Holy Spirit. Then, in 3:6-9, he discusses the Abrahamic covenant, refuting the way that false teachers were misappropriating the rite of circumcision, which did not contribute to Abraham's standing before God. In 3:10-14, he introduces the curse of the Law, explaining that Christ became a curse for us. There is deeply harrowing Old Testament imagery here that we will get to in just a few paragraphs. Afterward, in 3:15-18, he brings back his reference to Abraham and the promise the Lord gave him in Genesis 12, entering into a profound interaction between the covenant of faith and the covenant of law. Faith says, "God will." Law says, "You will." You either live by one or the other. Take your pick.

In Habakkuk 2, God tells the prophet to write the vision he receives plainly so that those who see it may run away from the destruction about to occur. God also informs the prophet in this same message that "the righteous shall live by his faith" (Hab. 2:4b). This is an amazing statement showing that the path of faith is the one which the faithful walk upon, not the path of self-righteousness (which only leads to destruction).

So the path the Christian walks is of faith, not of works, and this faith is founded upon the only one who walked perfectly, Jesus Christ. As mentioned before, there is some deep imagery you will encounter in this passage. This instance occurs in v. 13, a verse in which Paul is calling back to the following passage from the Torah:

And if a man has committed a crime punishable by death and he is put to death, and you hang him on a tree, his body shall not remain all night on the tree, but you shall bury him the same day, for a hanged man is cursed by God. You shall not defile your land that the Lord your God is giving you for an inheritance.

- Deuteronomy 21:22-23

"A hanged man is cursed by God." This statement is absolutely breathtaking when you consider Christ being that very hanged man. In the context of Galatians 3:10-18, this statement figuratively reads, then, "Christ, when hung on the cross, was cursed by God."

He suffered the punishment of a vile Roman criminal, of which he was clearly innocent. Even the pagan governor Pilate knew this (Matt. 27:24). Yet, even worse than that death was Christ being forsaken by the Father. He sacrificed himself in this way so that you and I may know God not only as wrathful but as merciful.

CHAPTER 8: A CRIMINAL'S DEATH | *Galatians 3:10-18*

PASSAGE

GALATIANS 3:10-18

¹⁰ For all who rely on works of the law are under a curse; for it is written, "Cursed be everyone who does not abide by all things written in the Book of the Law, and do them." ¹¹ Now it is evident that no one is justified before God by the law, for "The righteous shall live by faith." ¹² But the law is not of faith, rather "The one who does them shall live by them." ¹³ Christ redeemed us from the curse of the law by becoming a curse for us—for it is written, "Cursed is everyone who is hanged on a tree"— ¹⁴ so that in Christ Jesus the blessing of Abraham might come to the Gentiles, so that we might receive the promised Spirit through faith. ¹⁵ To give a human example, brothers: even with a man-made covenant, no one annuls it or adds to it once it has been ratified. ¹⁶ Now the promises were made to Abraham and to his offspring. It does not say, "And to offsprings," referring to many, but referring to one, "And to your offspring," who is Christ. ¹⁷ This is what I mean: the law, which came 430 years afterward, does not annul a covenant previously ratified by God, so as to make the promise void. ¹⁸ For if the inheritance comes by the law, it no longer comes by promise; but God gave it to Abraham by a promise.

INSIGHTS AND EXPOSITION

v. 10

"under a curse"

> Those who rely on their accomplishment of the Law are cursed (Deut. 27:26). Their status is opposite those of faith (Gal. 3:9).

v. 11

"Justified"

> To be justified is to be declared or made righteous before God.

"The righteous shall live by faith"

> Cited from Hab. 2:4, also in Rom. 1:17.

v. 12

"The law is not of faith"

> 1) The Law shall not be viewed as congruent with the path of faith. 2) Many heard the Law but did not abide by it, making their hearing void (Rom. 2:13). The same can be said of the gospel today.

"The one ... by them"

> Cited from Lev. 18:5.

CHAPTER 8: A CRIMINAL'S DEATH | *Galatians 3:10-18*

v. 13

"Christ redeemed us"

"Redeemed" is from *exagorazō*, which speaks of purchasing a slave's liberty. Through Christ's blood, you and I have been redeemed from the curse of the Law.

"Cursed is ... a tree"

In Israel, when a criminal would be executed for their crime, their body would usually be suspended from a tree for all to see until sundown. This symbolized rejection by God. For the unbelieving Jews, Christ could not have been the promised Messiah given the nature of his own hanging. This is why Paul can write that those who call Christ accursed are not of God, but only those who call him Lord (1 Cor. 12:3).

v. 14

"so that ... the Gentiles"

The blessing of Abraham that has come to the Gentiles is delivered through Christ and received by faith.

"the promised Holy Spirit"
>The Holy Spirit is a seal of the believer's faith; therefore, the blessing of Abraham is expressly seen in the believer's possession of the Spirit.

v. 15

"To give a human example"
>Gr.: *kata anthrōpon lego*, literally, "I speak as a man." Paul is trying to convey a spiritual reality using human terms.

"brothers"
>Paul addresses the Galatians as brothers, softly taking them along to see the analogy he is now presenting.

"covenant"
>Gr.: *diathēkē*, a binding agreement. Paul is stating that even man-made covenants are binding. The reader should then ask, "How much more binding are God-made covenants?" "no one ... been ratified" - Covenants shall not be amended once they have been sealed. The New Covenant, *the gospel*, cannot have anything added to it.

v. 16

"Now the ... his offspring"
>The promise that God gave to Abraham was not fulfilled in the giving of the Law, but was fulfilled in the New Covenant.

"And to ... 'is Christ'"
>Christ is the one sent by God, the very author of salvation, to fulfill the promises given to Abraham. Those who anticipated Christ before he came and those who believe in him now are saved.

v. 17

"the law ... promise void"
>1) Paul's central thesis in this verse is that the Abrahamic covenant was not annulled at the giving of the Law. The Law was an intermediary between Abraham and Christ. 2) Paul's intention in stating that the Law came 430 years after the Abrahamic covenant is to show that there were those who were in right standing with God prior to the establishment of the Mosaic covenant.

v. 18

"For if ... a promise"

Is an inheritance earned? No, it is given. So, the New Covenant is not of works but of grace. This is further emphasized in the second half of the verse in which Paul states, "but God gave it to Abraham by a promise." The verb "gave" is translated from the perfect tense verb, *charizomai*, which means to give graciously.

CHAPTER 8: A CRIMINAL'S DEATH | *Galatians 3:10-18*

KEY CONCEPTS

USE OF THE OLD TESTAMENT

4. Why do you think it was important for Paul to incorporate Old Testament passages within his argument?

5. What does "Cursed is everyone who is hanged on a tree" mean?

THE NEW COVENANT

6. What does it mean to call oneself redeemed?

7. How did Christ redeem us and what did he redeem us from?

APPLICATION

You and I stand cursed before God on account of our sins. The curses that are listed in Deuteronomy 28:15-68 should be given to us and more; yet, on account of Christ, we are blessed far more abundantly than our feeble minds can fathom.

It should be a Christian's desire for all people to hear of the unfathomable riches of Christ before they die, receiving a chance to enjoy the inheritance of salvation—something that is not owed to us but is nevertheless offered to all people through Jesus (Gal. 3:14; Eph. 3:8). So, as you wrap up your study of Galatians 3:10-18, write down the names of those in your life whom you should preach the gospel to so they, too, may abide in Christ:

_____

_____

_____

_____

_____

_____

_____

_____

NOTES

CHAPTER 8: A CRIMINAL'S DEATH | *Galatians 3:10-18*

CHAPTER 9:

UNITY IN CHRIST

GALATIANS 3:19-29

SPARK A CONNECTION

1. Have you ever felt stuck in a situation, as if you would never be able to get out? Perhaps your engine died while on the freeway or you ran out of money before the month's end. Describe this experience.

---

2. Were you set free from that situation? If so, how did that liberation occur? Maybe a tow truck came to your rescue or a friend offered much-needed financial help.

---

3. Discuss: If you are in a group, share your experiences with one another.

CHAPTER 9: UNITY IN CHRIST | *Galatians 3:19-29*

BACKGROUND AND CONTEXT

Humans are inherently sinful. One needs to look no further than their own thought life to see the verity of this fact. Would you want all your thoughts projected onto a screen for your whole family and church to see? Probably not.

Given our fallen nature, we need to abide by laws so our societies can be kept in proper order. Through the observance of these laws, we are withheld from performing offensive acts such as stealing from a convenience store, assaulting an innocent bystander or spreading illicit content online. There are more laws, rules and regulations in your country than you can conceive of. They have all been enacted to ensure that humans do not violate or exploit one another in a given interaction.

Just as human laws have been enacted because of sin, God's Law was enacted because of sin. His Law has been revealed to us so that the evil within may be exposed. Upon exposure, the sinner must look to Christ for cleansing, for it is only according to his righteousness that the accusations of the enemy may be defeated. Consider the way Joshua the high priest was clothed in Zechariah 2:

Then he showed me Joshua the high priest standing before the angel of the Lord, and Satan standing at his right hand to accuse him. And the Lord said to Satan, "The Lord rebuke you, O Satan! The

Lord who has chosen Jerusalem rebuke you! Is not this a brand plucked from the fire?" Now Joshua was standing before the angel, clothed with filthy garments. And the angel said to those who were standing before him, "Remove the filthy garments from him." And to him he said, "Behold, I have taken your iniquity away from you, and I will clothe you with pure vestments."... Hear now, O Joshua the high priest, you and your friends who sit before you, for they are men who are a sign: behold, I will bring my servant the Branch. For behold, on the stone that I have set before Joshua, on a single stone with seven eyes, I will engrave its inscription, declares the Lord of hosts, and I will remove the iniquity of this land in a single day. In that day, declares the Lord of hosts, every one of you will invite his neighbor to come under his vine and under his fig tree."

- Zechariah 3:1-4, 8-10

On his own merit, Joshua could not refute the accusation of Satan. God needed to step in as his advocate and declare him to be a "brand plucked from the fire," holy and righteous in his sight. For you and I to be clothed in such pure vestments, we need to be united with Christ. This unity with our Lord does not only have vertical consequences but horizontal consequences too, as we will see in the passage to come. Through our justification, we join Christ's church, a body of believers consecrated and unified to be the hands and feet of Jesus in this world.

CHAPTER 9: UNITY IN CHRIST | *Galatians 3:19-29*

PASSAGE

GALATIANS 3:19-29

¹⁹ Why then the law? It was added because of transgressions, until the offspring should come to whom the promise had been made, and it was put in place through angels by an intermediary. ²⁰ Now an intermediary implies more than one, but God is one.

²¹ Is the law then contrary to the promises of God? Certainly not! For if a law had been given that could give life, then righteousness would indeed be by the law. ²² But the Scripture imprisoned everything under sin, so that the promise by faith in Jesus Christ might be given to those who believe.

²³ Now before faith came, we were held captive under the law, imprisoned until the coming faith would be revealed. ²⁴ So then, the law was our guardian until Christ came, in order that we might be justified by faith. ²⁵ But now that faith has come, we are no longer under a guardian, ²⁶ for in Christ Jesus you are all sons of God, through faith. ²⁷ For as many of you as were baptized into Christ have put on Christ. ²⁸ There is neither Jew nor Greek, there is neither slave nor free, there is no male and female, for you are all one in Christ Jesus. ²⁹ And if you are Christ's, then you are Abraham's offspring, heirs according to promise.

INSIGHTS AND EXPOSITION

v. 19

"Why then the law?"

> Torah was not given as a means of salvation but as a means of exposure. This is why Paul can say it was added "because of transgressions," shining the spotlight on our sins and indicating humanity's need for a savior. This was a necessary explanation given the Galatians' Gentile heritage. They had very little prior exposure to the Law.

"it was ... an intermediary"

> The Mosaic covenant was given by angels (Heb. 2:2). The display that accompanied the giving of the Law was a theophany of fear and fury (Ex. 19:24). Yet, the giving of the Abrahamic covenant was peaceful. The Lord made this covenant with man by himself, not by intermediaries (Gen. 12:1-3; Gen. 15:1-7; 18:1-33).

v. 20

"Now an ... is one"

> This is one of the most obscure verses in all of Scripture. It seems like Paul is contrasting

the Abrahamic and Mosaic covenants in a different way. Abraham was not an active party in the covenant God established with him. He had no duties to attain righteousness. In the Mosaic covenant, however, humanity was responsible for upholding the Law; God and humanity were both active parties. So, the difference here is that Abraham did not need to fulfill a set of standards to be right with God. It was God who declared him righteous, and God alone.

v. 21

"Is the ... of God?"

The Law is not contrary to God's promise to Abraham. It does not somehow cancel the promise out.

"Certainly not!"

This is a common phrase Paul uses to refute aberrant and faulty logic (Rom. 6:1-2; 7:13).

"For if ... the law"

The Law cannot save; however, if it could, then it would contradict the way of salvation God ordained in the Abrahamic covenant.

v. 22

"imprisoned"

> Gr.: *sunkleiō*, to lock up securely. This is a potent word that casts an image of being stuck in a room with no way of escape.

"so that ... who believe"

> Through the knowledge of sin we may receive the knowledge of Christ.

v. 23

"Now before faith came"

> There is a definite article before the word "faith" in the original language, indicating that this faith is not a generic one but a particular faith in Christ that can be traced back to a single point in history.

"we were ... be revealed"

> Paul repeats this idea of sinners being held captive under the tyranny of the Law. But, now that Christ has come, we are set free.

CHAPTER 9: UNITY IN CHRIST | *Galatians 3:19-29*

v. 24

"So then ... by faith"

> The popular rendering of this verse comes from the KJV. The Law serving as a guardian is translated there as "tutor." The Law, then, is a schoolmaster who points their students to the cross. Gr.: *paidagōgos*, a supervisor, often an educated slave who watched over the children of their master until they were of age.

vv. 25-26

"But now ... a guardian"

> Building upon v. 24, Paul says that Christians are no longer under this guardian.

"for in ... through faith"

> Our guardian no longer watches over us. We have attained full maturity through the belief granted to us in Christ. We are now sons of God through faith. There are occasions in the New Testament where humans are referred to as children of God generally (Acts 17:28); but, Paul is speaking of us being sons or children of God in a salvific manner.

v. 27

"For as ... on Christ"

>Through water baptism, we have publicly declared our union with Christ. This verse does not contradict Paul's assertion that salvation is by faith alone. Instead, baptism outwardly symbolizes an inward reality.

v. 28

"There is ... Christ Jesus"

>1) Drawing upon the societal barriers and distinctions of his day, Paul is asserting that these distinctions do not have a say as it regards one's salvation. All who believe can come to Christ. Jew or Greek, you are free in Christ (Acts 10:35); slave or free, you are welcome; male or female, you are free indeed. 2) The Christian church elevated women's status in the ancient world. A man submitting to the fleshly desires of his wife would have been unheard of during this time period (1 Cor. 7:4). Yet, some have used v. 28 to claim that there are no distinctions between genders in the kingdom of God, therefore making all

sorts of assertions concerning gender identity and the role of men and women in the home and church. As evidenced by other passages, such distinctions have been put in place by God for his divine purposes and are not annulled by the New Covenant (Gen. 1:27; 1 Cor. 7:1-5, 11:3; 1 Tim. 2:8-15; Titus 2:3-5).

v. 29

"And if ... to promise"

Bringing back his claim concerning sonship in v. 26, Paul concludes this portion of his argument by stating we are Abraham's offspring. We are the ones who receive his inheritance. This is no longer a result of Law or ethnic heritage, but of grace and faith.

KEY CONCEPTS

THE FUNCTION OF THE LAW

4. Why did God give humanity the Law?

5. How does the Law expose the sin of our hearts?

6. Based upon your previous answers, is preaching the moral standards of the Law necessary when giving a gospel presentation to an unbeliever? Why?

CHAPTER 9: UNITY IN CHRIST | *Galatians 3:19-29*

SALVATION FOR ALL

7. In context of chapter 3, what does verse 28 mean? How does it apply to the lives of all believers?

8. To what promise are Christians heirs? What do we inherit? (v. 29)

APPLICATION

As we have learned, the Law is our guardian, pointing out our sins with one hand and pointing to the cure with the other. It is through the Law that we have revelation of our sinful state and separation from God. It was our Lord who said,

For I tell you, unless your righteousness exceeds that of the scribes and Pharisees, you will never enter the kingdom of heaven.

- Matthew 5:20

The only way in which our righteousness can exceed that of the legalists is through faith in Christ. If there was a theme to the book of Galatians, this would be it. Even so, we who call ourselves followers of Christ must abide to a higher moral standard than even that of the Law requires.

The Law calls us a murderer if we kill someone in cold blood, but Christ calls us a murderer if we have anger in our hearts (Matt. 5:21-22). The Law calls us an adulterer if we sleep with another's spouse, but Christs calls us an adulterer if we simply lust with our eyes (Matt. 5:27-28). The Law permits us to divorce our spouse for ambiguous reasons, but Christ calls us to live faithfully to our vows (Matt. 5:31-32, 19:1-9; 1 Cor. 7:10-11).

These examples could go on ad infinitum. The bottom line is that living by faith requires a higher standard of integrity than living by the Law. For believers, the Spirit of God will enable us to live as Jesus did.

CHAPTER 9: UNITY IN CHRIST | *Galatians 3:19-29*

NOTES

CHAPTER 10:

LABORING IN VAIN

———

GALATIANS 4:1-20

SPARK A CONNECTION

1. In ministry, has someone whom you invested in abandoned your church or organization? Perhaps it was a member of your worship team, or a youth you counseled weekly. If so, what events led to their departure?

2. How did their departure make you feel? Did you ever consider all of your hardwork to be meaningless?

3. Discuss: Share your thoughts with those around you. Note any similarities or differences between your respective experiences.

CHAPTER 10: LABORING IN VAIN | *Galatians 4:1-20*

BACKGROUND AND CONTEXT

Just as you and I may have experienced the disappointment of losing one whom we discipled, the Apostle Paul experienced this on a grander scale. For Paul, after having spent precious time among the Galatian assemblies, to see these believers abandon the gospel for a false alternative was perplexing at best and anguishing at worst. To express this pain and discontentment, Paul will rely upon his analogy of a formerly supervised young person from 3:23-26.

In this set of verses, Paul described the Law as a guardian until Christ. By this, he meant that the Law acts as an educated slave whose responsibility was to teach the Greek language to the children of their Roman master and ensure their safety. After spending a select number of years under their guardian, the young person would be emancipated. So, the analogy that Paul is articulating here pictures the Law as the one who trained us to be made free in Christ.

Now, since the Galatian believers have already been set free, Paul is astonished that they are returning to their guardian. This may remind you of the Hebrews grumbling in the wilderness:

They set out from Elim, and all the congregation of the people of Israel came to the wilderness of Sin, which is between Elim and Sinai, on the fifteenth day of the second month after they had departed from the land of Egypt. And the whole congregation of the people of Israel grumbled against Moses and Aaron in the wilderness, and the people of Israel said to them, "Would that we had died by the hand of the Lord in the land of Egypt, when we sat by the meat pots and ate bread to the full, for you have brought us out into this wilderness to kill this whole assembly with hunger."

- Exodus 16:1-3

In their dissolute lack of gratitude, the newly emancipated Hebrews expressed resentment toward God their liberator. They accused him of attempting to kill the assembly of the people with hunger as they wandered in the wilderness. Could not the Lord provide food for them? In a similar fashion, the Galatians are returning back to the Law in an effort to regain some semblance of righteousness, without which they would perish. Yet, as we have learned through our study, true righteousness is not the result of a combination of faith and works but is solely provided by God, just as the Abrahamic covenant was.

The Galatians would have once done anything for Paul's sake, even gouging out their own eyes so that they may restore his sight (4:15). Despite this former symbol of fidelity, these believers view Paul as a former ally and present enemy (4:16). The bewitching of the Judaizers is in full effect, and Paul is doing whatever he can to bring those whom he labored over out of their trance.

CHAPTER 10: LABORING IN VAIN | *Galatians 4:1-20*

PASSAGE

GALATIANS 4:1-20

¹ I mean that the heir, as long as he is a child, is no different from a slave, though he is the owner of everything, ² but he is under guardians and managers until the date set by his father. ³ In the same way we also, when we were children, were enslaved to the elementary principles of the world. ⁴ But when the fullness of time had come, God sent forth his Son, born of woman, born under the law, ⁵ to redeem those who were under the law, so that we might receive adoption as sons. ⁶ And because you are sons, God has sent the Spirit of his Son into our hearts, crying, "Abba! Father!" ⁷ So you are no longer a slave, but a son, and if a son, then an heir through God.

⁸ Formerly, when you did not know God, you were enslaved to those that by nature are not gods. ⁹ But now that you have come to know God, or rather to be known by God, how can you turn back again to the weak and worthless elementary principles of the world, whose slaves you want to be once more? ¹⁰ You observe days and months and seasons and years! ¹¹ I am afraid I may have labored over you in vain.

¹² Brothers, I entreat you, become as I am, for I also have become as you are. You did me no wrong. ¹³ You know it was because of a bodily ailment that I preached the gospel to you at first, ¹⁴ and though my condition was a trial to you, you did not scorn or despise

me, but received me as an angel of God, as Christ Jesus. ⁱ⁵ What then has become of your blessedness? For I testify to you that, if possible, you would have gouged out your eyes and given them to me.
ⁱ⁶ Have I then become your enemy by telling you the truth? ⁱ⁷ They make much of you, but for no good purpose. They want to shut you out, that you may make much of them. ⁱ⁸ It is always good to be made much of for a good purpose, and not only when I am present with you, ⁱ⁹ my little children, for whom I am again in the anguish of childbirth until Christ is formed in you! ²⁰ I wish I could be present with you now and change my tone, for I am perplexed about you.

CHAPTER 10: LABORING IN VAIN | *Galatians 4:1-20*

INSIGHTS AND EXPOSITION

vv. 1-2

"I mean ... his father"

Paul's meaning in these two verses is to apply the analogy of the guarded child to the life of the believer. In Greece, a boy would be guarded until he was 18-years-old, then he would assume special responsibilities to his city-state. Likewise, in Roman society, a boy or girl would take their toys and sacrifice them to the gods as a symbol of entering adulthood (1 Cor. 13:11). Before these children were emancipated, they were the equivalent of the slave who guarded them. If a Christian goes back to the Law, then they are not walking in the emancipation available to them, reducing their status to one who is bound (3:23).

v. 3

"elementary principles"

In Col. 2:8, Paul speaks of the elementary principles of the world. He poses them in opposition to Christ. These principles are human philosophy, tradition and false religion.

vv. 4-5

"But when ... had come"

> The Law has served its purpose according to God's providential calendar.

"God sent ... the law"

> This phrase in v. 4b speaks to Christ's incarnation. We understand that Christ was *vera homo, vera Deus*, meaning truly man and truly God. In his human embodiment, he was no less God than he was before (John 1:1-5). He was "born of a woman," symbolizing his humanity (Is. 7:14). He was also born "under the law" that he might fulfill it (Rom. 8:3-4).

"to redeem ... as sons"

> We who were under the Law need liberation from our imprisonment. Through Christ, we not only receive liberation but adoption. The adopted inherits all the rights and privileges of a natural-born child though they were brought in from elsewhere.

v. 6

"And because ... 'Abba! Father!'"

1) God the Father has sent the Spirit of his Son into our hearts. This speaks to the Triunity of God. 2) "Abba" is the Aramaic diminutive term for Father. It likely carried loving connotations; however, it is not exactly the equivalent of the English term, "Daddy," since both children and adults used "Abba" when referring to their fathers. Nevertheless, we have inherited sonship through Christ Jesus, allowing us to call God our Father (Rom. 8:14-16).

v. 7

"So you ... through God"

Paul sums up his argument but does not provide a direct end. Instead, he lets it float into the following verses.

vv. 8-9

"Formerly"

This is the third time Paul speaks of the Galatians' enslaved state (3:23; 4:1).

"not gods"

    The Galatians were former pagan worshipers. They honored idols, which in Paul's terms cannot be regarded as gods.

"But now ... once more?"

    How could the Galatians return to the gods, traditions and philosophies they once served. Their alteration of the gospel has rendered Christ's sacrifice empty for their sakes.

v. 10

"You observe ... and years!"

    Paul is now referring to the Jewish ceremonial calendar. "Days" refers to Sabbath and feast days; "months" refers to routine celebrations that followed a monthly cycle (cf. Is. 1:14); "seasons" refers to festivals such as the Passover; "years" refers to the recurring years of Jubilee (Lev. 25).

v. 11

"I am ... in vain"

    Paul expresses his fear that his work among the Galatian churches has been for nothing given their abandonment of the gospel.

CHAPTER 10: LABORING IN VAIN | *Galatians 4:1-20*

vv. 12-15

"Brothers, I entreat you"

In an extension of warm persuasion, Paul's tone is now changing. He is not speaking harshly to the Judaizers or Galatians but is speaking to the congregations in a loving manner.

"become as I am"

This is in regards to dying to the Law (2:19).

"for I also have become as you are"

Paul was once a zealous Jew who sought salvation through works of the Law (Phil. 3:4-6).

"bodily ailment"

We are not sure what Paul's bodily ailment was. We can assume, though, that it was a temporary malady since he came to them as a result of contracting the condition.

"and though ... Christ Jesus"

The Galatians received Paul as Christ himself. After all, Paul was an apostle of Christ, so he spoke as authoritatively as our Lord himself. Paul does not denounce their honorable reception of him, further re-establishing his identity as an apostle.

v. 15

"What then ... to me"

> Paul may have been using a common adage in his day. Gouging one's eyes out for the sake of another was not literal, but figurative. Some scholars speculate that he uses this phrase given his poor eyesight, which is why he wrote with such large letters (Gal. 6:11).

v. 16

"Have I ... the truth?"

> Just as Jesus mourned over Jerusalem's refusal of him (Luke 13:34), Paul mourns over Galatia's refusal.

vv. 17-19

"They make much of you"

> This phrase can speak of a male attempting to suit a potential mate.

CHAPTER 10: LABORING IN VAIN | *Galatians 4:1-20*

"It is ... good purpose"
> Making much of someone can be for good, just as the Galatians made much of Paul when he initially ministered to them.

"my little children"
> Gr.: *teknion*, referring to a small child. This term was used affectionately.

"childbirth"
> Elsewhere, Paul uses motherly imagery to describe his apostolic labor (1 Thess. 2:7).

"until Christ is formed in you!"
> Paul's goal is the formation of Christ in the churches he oversees.

v. 20

"perplexed"
> Gr.: *aporoumai*, to be at a loss or one's wit's end.

KEY CONCEPTS

ELEMENTARY PRINCIPLES

4. What is Paul referring to when he mentions the "elementary principles of the world?" (v. 3, 9)

5. In verses 9 and 10, Paul relates these elementary principles to Jewish practices. How are these two concepts connected?

CHAPTER 10: LABORING IN VAIN | *Galatians 4:1-20*

PAUL'S EXAMPLE

6. What does Paul mean when he entreats the Galatians to become as he is? (v. 12) What characteristics are they to embody?

_____

_____

_____

_____

7. We are to honor God more than man. So why, then, was it right for the Galatians to receive Paul as Christ himself? (v. 14)

_____

_____

_____

_____

8. Having worked through much of Paul's argument in his epistle to the Galatians, what is his overall purpose in contrasting slaves and free people?

_____

_____

_____

_____

APPLICATION

In Christ, you have been set free from the curse of sin and death. It is because of the work of those who labor for you that you heard the gospel and are now justified in God's sight. Just as the Galatians received Paul in honor, we, too, must recognize the work of our elders.

Let the elders who rule well be considered worthy of double honor, especially those who labor in preaching and teaching. For the Scripture says, "You shall not muzzle an ox when it treads out the grain," and, "The laborer deserves his wages."

- 1 Timothy 5:17-18

Are you willing to take the clothes off your back and place them upon your pastors if they are in dire need of assistance? Are you not only willing to do so for them, but to do so for any member of Christ's body who lacks? (Jas. 2:14-17)

Take a moment to allow the Lord to search your heart. We may often think we are prepared to sacrifice everything for the sake of the brethren but have we truly considered the weight of this calling and responsibility? (Jn. 15:13) May we be prepared to give up all our possessions so that no member of Christ's body is found lacking.

CHAPTER 10: LABORING IN VAIN | *Galatians 4:1-20*

NOTES

CHAPTER 11:

CHILDREN OF PROMISE

GALATIANS 4:21-5:1

SPARK A CONNECTION

1. Recall a time in your life when you were fully dependent upon God to work a miracle on your behalf. Maybe you did not meet any of the requirements for a job your applied for, causing you to rely solely on God's miraculous favor for the position. Whatever your experience may be, briefly describe what you were trusting in the Lord for.

2. How did you see God's hand move on your behalf?

3. Discuss: Share your story of God's favor with those around you, encouraging each other to rely upon the Lord for supernatural provision.

CHAPTER 11: CHILDREN OF PROMISE | *Galatians 4:21-5:1*

BACKGROUND AND CONTEXT

Galatians 4:21-5:1 is a bit complex. As we have seen before, the overall message of Galatians is abundantly clear; however, Paul's inspired argument flows in and out of deep wells of biblical truth, requiring the reader to do some deep diving if they desire to absorb all that lies beneath the surface. Even the Apostle Peter admitted so:

And count the patience of our Lord as salvation, just as our beloved brother Paul also wrote to you according to the wisdom given him, as he does in all his letters when he speaks in them of these matters. There are some things in them that are hard to understand, which the ignorant and unstable twist to their own destruction, as they do the other Scriptures.

- 2 Peter 3:15-16

In the passage to come, Paul presents a rich illustration concerning the children of the promise and the conflict between Hagar and Sarah found in Genesis. The saga of this conflict begins in Genesis 12, which we have discussed before, where the Lord promises Abram that he will make a great nation out of him and that the land of Canaan will belong to his offspring. At the time of this revelation Abram is 75-years-old and his wife, Sarai, is 65—well beyond childbearing age. Yet, the promise of the Lord stood for the following 25 years as it awaited its fruition.

The narrative picks up again in Genesis 15 where God forms a covenant with Abram. Here, Abram cries out to the Lord, proclaiming that God has not yet given him a son. Abram is concerned that the promise God granted him will be left to his only heir, a servant named Eliezer. God responds to Abram by telling him that he will give him his very own son to inherit his promise. Then in the next chapter, we find a perplexed Sarai. Because she has yet to see the promise fulfilled in her womb, Sarai hastily takes matters into her own hands by asking Abram to go into her servant, Hagar. The much younger Hagar bears the couple a son, stirring up jealously within Sarai's heart.

Sarai mistreats her newly impregnated servant, and as a result of such maltreatment, Hagar flees for the wilderness. While this runaway slave mournfully sits by a spring of water, an angel of the Lord appears to her. Through this messenger, the Lord commands her to return to Sarai and later informs her that the son growing within her belly will be called Ishmael:

"Behold, you are pregnant and shall bear a son. You shall call his name Ishmael, because the Lord has listened to your affliction. He shall be a wild donkey of a man, his hand against everyone and everyone's hand against him, and he shall dwell over against all his kinsmen."

- Genesis 16:11-12

CHAPTER 11: CHILDREN OF PROMISE | *Galatians 4:21-5:1*

In the entirety of the Hebrew Bible, this is the only instance a woman personally interacts with the Lord. Of all women, God chooses to listen to the affliction of a castaway slave, sending her his word in response to her anguish. Reacting to the weight of the revelation she just received, Hagar responds with a worshipful heart:

So she called the name of the Lord who spoke to her, "You are a God of seeing," for she said, "Truly here I have seen him who looks after me." Therefore the well was called Beer-lahai-roi; it lies between Kadesh and Bered.

- Genesis 16:13-14

In the next chapter of Genesis, God promises that the 90-year-old Sarai, who is now called Sarah, will bear a son for Abraham, who is 99. Upon hearing this incredible promise in Genesis 18, Sarah finds it so absurd given her age that she laughs. So, when God indeed blessed Abraham's seed and Sarah's womb, their son was named Isaac, which means laughter.

The Lord visited Sarah as he had said, and the Lord did to Sarah as he had promised. And Sarah conceived and bore Abraham a son in his old age at the time of which God had spoken to him. Abraham called the name of his son who was born to him, whom Sarah bore him, Isaac. And Abraham circumcised his son

Isaac when he was eight days old, as God had commanded him. Abraham was a hundred years old when his son Isaac was born to him. And Sarah said, "God has made laughter for me; everyone who hears will laugh over me." And she said, "Who would have said to Abraham that Sarah would nurse children? Yet I have borne him a son in his old age."

- Genesis 21:1-7

While the Lord made Ishmael into a great nation, it was Isaac who was the heir of the promise. Now, as far as Paul's illustration goes, we are children and heirs of the promise from the line of Isaac, not the line of Ishmael. As a result of this sonship, we inherit the covenant that God made with Abraham, and it is for this reason that we and the Galatians are not to submit again to a yoke of slavery—the Law—but live in the freedom we have inherited through Christ.

CHAPTER 11: CHILDREN OF PROMISE | *Galatians 4:21-5:1*

PASSAGE

GALATIANS 4:21-5:1

²¹ Tell me, you who desire to be under the law, do you not listen to the law? ²² For it is written that Abraham had two sons, one by a slave woman and one by a free woman. ²³ But the son of the slave was born according to the flesh, while the son of the free woman was born through promise. ²⁴ Now this may be interpreted allegorically: these women are two covenants. One is from Mount Sinai, bearing children for slavery; she is Hagar. ²⁵ Now Hagar is Mount Sinai in Arabia; she corresponds to the present Jerusalem, for she is in slavery with her children. ²⁶ But the Jerusalem above is free, and she is our mother. ²⁷ For it is written,

> *"Rejoice, O barren one who does not bear;*
>
> *break forth and cry aloud, you who are not in labor!*
>
> *For the children of the desolate one will be more*
>
> *than those of the one who has a husband."*

²⁸ Now you, brothers, like Isaac, are children of promise. ²⁹ But just as at that time he who was born according to the flesh persecuted him who was born according to the Spirit, so also it is now. ³⁰ But what does the Scripture say? "Cast out the slave woman and her son, for the son of the slave woman shall not inherit with the son of the free woman." ³¹ So, brothers, we are not children of the slave but of the free woman.

¹ For freedom Christ has set us free; stand firm therefore, and do not submit again to a yoke of slavery.

INSIGHTS AND EXPOSITION

v. 21

"Tell me ... the law?"

> Continuing his plea for the Galatians to stand in freedom, Paul asks them if they truly know the Law, for if they truly knew the Law, they would not be departing from the gospel.

v. 22

"For it ... free woman"

> Paul reminds the Galatians that Abraham had a son through the flesh and a son through the promise. From which line do they descend? (Jn. 8:31-38)

v. 23

"But the ... through promise"

> One son of Abraham was born through a slave woman and the other was born through a free woman. The son of the slave woman was born according to the flesh and the son of the freewoman was born according to the promise.

CHAPTER 11: CHILDREN OF PROMISE | *Galatians 4:21-5:1*

vv. 24-26

"interpreted allegorically"

Gr.: *allēgoreō*, to speak allegorically. Paul here is saying that the historical story of Sarah and Hagar is a spiritual sign of the gospel.

"Hagar is Mount Sinai"

1) Hagar's son, Ishmael, bore descendants that dwelled in Arabia. 2) Spiritually, Hagar and Ishmael represent the Law, which was given at Sinai.

"the present Jerusalem"

This city represents the continuing practice of the Law.

"the Jerusalem above"

This Jerusalem differs from the present Jerusalem in that it is filled with followers of Christ, rather than followers of the Law.

v. 27

"For it ... 'a husband'"
> This verse is a reference to Is. 54:1 which was originally written for the inspiration of the Jews amidst the Babylonian exile. Applied in the New Covenant, this verse indicates that the children of the promise will outnumber the children of the flesh (Christians will outnumber Jews).

vv. 28-31

"so also it is now"
> Just as Ishmael's descendants persecuted Isaac's, so now the Jews persecute Christians.

"Cast out the slave woman"
> A reference to Gen. 21:8-14, Paul is stating that we must cast the Law away for the sake of the gospel.

CHAPTER 11: CHILDREN OF PROMISE | *Galatians 4:21-5:1*

"So, brothers ... free woman"

Referring to the Galatians as brethren, Paul sums up the point of his argument: do not live as children of the flesh, but as children of the promise, because children of the flesh will not reign as heirs with Christ, but only the children of the promise.

5:1

"For freedom ... of slavery"

Like any good preacher, Paul concludes this portion of his argument with an application. Since Christ set us free, we should refrain from submitting ourselves again to the yoke of slavery (Rom. 6:17-19). Instead, we should only put on the yoke of Christ (Matt. 11:28-30).

KEY CONCEPTS

CHILDREN OF THE PROMISE

4. What does it mean to be a child of the promise?

5. Underline every use of the words "free" and "slave" in 4:21-5:1. What are the differences between those whom Paul calls free and those whom Paul calls slaves?

CHAPTER 11: CHILDREN OF PROMISE | *Galatians 4:21-5:1*

STANDING FIRM

6. How can you stand firm in the freedom Christ has purchased for you?

7. Read Matthew 11:25-30. How have you found rest for your soul in Christ?

APPLICATION

What a better exhortation for this chapter than the one found in Galatians 5:1? As a believer in Christ, you must stand firm in the freedom that he has given you. This freedom was purchased for you by his blood. His beaten body hung on the cross, cursed and bearing the wrath of God, so that you may experience liberty, forgiveness and everlasting joy. Through Jesus' resurrection, you will be resurrected (1 Pet. 1:3). So rejoice and be glad! Your humble king has sacrificed his life for an unworthy subject.

Perhaps you currently find yourself struggling to walk in Christ's liberty and forgiveness because of ongoing sin. Do not fear. You are not alone in this struggle. Know that your fight against sin is evidence that the Lord is working in your life. If you were not in Christ, then you would have no remorse for your ongoing habits of sin; but, because you are in him, you understand your constant need to repent and correct course just like the Galatians.

Consider reading the following hymn. May you experience peace in knowing that all of God's children are prone to wander, but it is his love that takes our hearts like a fetter and binds them to himself.

Come, Thou Fount of every blessing,
Tune my heart to sing Thy grace;
Streams of mercy, never ceasing,
Call for songs of loudest praise.

CHAPTER 11: CHILDREN OF PROMISE | *Galatians 4:21-5:1*

Teach me some melodious sonnet,
Sung by flaming tongues above;
Praise the mount! I'm fixed upon it,
Mount of Thy redeeming love.

Here I raise my Ebenezer:
Here by Thy great help I've come;
And I hope, by Thy good pleasure,
Safely to arrive at home.
Jesus sought me when a stranger,
Wand'ring from the fold of God;
He, to rescue me from danger,
Interposed His precious blood.

Oh, to grace how great a debtor
Daily I'm constrained to be!
Let that grace now, like a fetter,
Bind my yielded heart to Thee.
Let me know Thee in Thy fullness;
Guide me by Thy mighty hand,
Till, transformed, in Thine own image
In Thy presence I shall stand.

- Asahel Nettleton, "Come Thou Fount of Every Blessing," 1813

NOTES

CHAPTER 11: CHILDREN OF PROMISE | *Galatians 4:21-5:1*

CHAPTER 12:

THE HOPE OF RIGHTEOUSNESS

GALATIANS 5:2-15

SPARK A CONNECTION

1. Have you ever felt separated from God? Perhaps you did not press into prayer as you should have, or you felt like God had abandoned you for an unknown reason. Write about this experience.

_____

_____

_____

_____

2. How were you redeemed from those feelings?

_____

_____

_____

3. Discuss: For those of us who have felt separated because of our own actions, the Galatians found themselves in a similar situation. Yet, Paul exhorted them—and exhorts us now—to turn back to the truth. How can we as believers bring others back to the truth of gospel living?

CHAPTER 12: THE HOPE OF RIGHTEOUSNESS | *Galatians 5:2-15*

BACKGROUND AND CONTEXT

It is easy for Christians to take advantage of the grace we live by. If we are honest with ourselves, we dabble with sin knowing full well that it is wrong. The reason for our persistence is often the knowledge that God's grace is not too shallow to fully cover the debt we owe. We abuse the freedom awarded to us, just like Israel did in the time of the judges:

In those days there was no king in Israel. Everyone did what was right in his own eyes.

- Judges 21:25

It is natural for humanity to abuse any sort of freedom it enjoys. If Micah 7:19 states that the Lord casts the sum of our sins into the depths of the sea, then the legalist's question is, "why live righteously?"

Progressing from his argument for justification by faith alone in Galatians 3 and 4, the Apostle Paul now endeavors to discuss matters of a righteous life. He is moving from doctrine to devotion, we might say—from orthodoxy to orthopraxy. Love, he argues, is the foundational, Law-fulfilling principle for disciples of Jesus to be known by. We are not to be marked by our own self-righteousness, but by faith working through love. This is why the legalist's inquiry can be so easily shut down. We are not living by Law, but by a higher standard: the Lord *himself*.

It is Christ's example that we follow. So, while we are called by the Law to not murder, we are called by Christ to not store up anger. It is not enough to simply live by the letter, but we ought to walk by the Spirit. This is Paul's emphasis in these final two chapters of Galatians. Here, he will once again confront the false teachers who have leavened the lump of the Galatian churches, exclaiming that he wishes they would not just circumcise themselves, but castrate themselves. This type of imagery conveys just how gravely serious Paul is about this matter. Holiness is not achieved by obeying ordinances; nor is it achieved by simply having a cognitive understanding of the truth. One must rely on Christ and his righteousness if they desire to one day stand faultless before the throne of God Almighty; they must not only recognize that Jesus is a cool guy with some fantastic insights but confess with their mouths that he is Lord and believe in their hearts that the Father raised him from the dead (Rom. 10:9)!

CHAPTER 12: THE HOPE OF RIGHTEOUSNESS | *Galatians 5:2-15*

While this salvific message is simple, it nevertheless requires much. During his earthly ministry, Jesus boldly proclaimed what following him would cost us:

Now when Jesus saw a crowd around him, he gave orders to go over to the other side. And a scribe came up and said to him, "Teacher, I will follow you wherever you go." And Jesus said to him, "Foxes have holes, and birds of the air have nests, but the Son of Man has nowhere to lay his head." Another of the disciples said to him, "Lord, let me first go and bury my father." And Jesus said to him, "Follow me, and leave the dead to bury their own dead."

- Matthew 8:18-22

Following Christ requires us to give everything for the sake of our Lord. However, we do not give in vain. We give because he gave; we love because he first loved us (1 Jn. 4:19).

PASSAGE

GALATIANS 5:2-15

² Look: I, Paul, say to you that if you accept circumcision, Christ will be of no advantage to you. ³ I testify again to every man who accepts circumcision that he is obligated to keep the whole law. ⁴ You are severed from Christ, you who would be justified by the law; you have fallen away from grace. ⁵ For through the Spirit, by faith, we ourselves eagerly wait for the hope of righteousness. ⁶ For in Christ Jesus neither circumcision nor uncircumcision counts for anything, but only faith working through love.

⁷ You were running well. Who hindered you from obeying the truth? ⁸ This persuasion is not from him who calls you. ⁹ A little leaven leavens the whole lump. ¹⁰ I have confidence in the Lord that you will take no other view, and the one who is troubling you will bear the penalty, whoever he is. ¹¹ But if I, brothers, still preach circumcision, why am I still being persecuted? In that case the offense of the cross has been removed. ¹² I wish those who unsettle you would emasculate themselves!

¹³ For you were called to freedom, brothers. Only do not use your freedom as an opportunity for the flesh, but through love serve one another. ¹⁴ For the whole law is fulfilled in one word: "You shall love your neighbor as yourself." ¹⁵ But if you bite and devour one another, watch out that you are not consumed by one another.

CHAPTER 12: THE HOPE OF RIGHTEOUSNESS | *Galatians 5:2-15*

INSIGHTS AND EXPOSITION

v. 2

"Look: I ... to you"

Paul reiterates that receiving circumcision nullifies the work of Christ. One might ask, "why does Paul say this when he had Timothy circumcised in Acts 16?" In Galatians, Paul is arguing against the theology of circumcision. The reason for circumcising Timothy was not theological but was for the sake of having a greater gospel witness among the Jews.

vv. 3-4

"I testify"

Gr.: *marturomai*, in this context this term pertains to strongly speaking or protesting against something.

"he is obligated to keep the whole law"

cf. Jas. 2:10

vv. 5-6

"the hope of righteousness"

While all who are Christ's are made righteous through their belief in him, Christians still await a coming glorification (Rom. 8:21, 30).

"only faith working through love"
> Love is the fulfillment of the Law. Paul will build upon this idea throughout this passage.

vv. 7-8

"You were running well"
> Paul frequently compares a Christian's walk to an athletic contest or race (1 Cor. 9:24-27; 2 Tim. 4:7).

"This persuasion ... calls you"
> The legalized gospel moving throughout the Galatian churches is not of God.

v. 9

"A little ... whole lump"
> Leaven is a figurative term regarding sinful teachings or practices. If it is present in the church, then its purity is at stake (Matt. 16:6-12).

v. 10

"I have ... he is"
> Paul has a firm conviction that the Galatians will return to the gospel of Christ. For the

false teachers, however, he asserts that they are destined for judgment.

v. 11

"But if I, brothers, still preach circumcision"
> If Paul still preached circumcision as he once did, then he would not face any persecution from the Jews. But because he does preach the gospel of faith, he is persecuted. It may have been that the Judaizers told the Galatians that Paul was a preacher of their gospel, thus bringing this necessary refutation from Paul.

v. 12

"emasculate themselves"
> Gr.: *apokoptō*, to cut off. Paul wishes those who advocate circumcision would just go all the way!

v. 13

"For you were called to freedom"
> The opposite of what Christians are called to is a life of bondage. We are not bound to the civil regulations and ceremonies of the Law.

"Only do ... one another"
> Paul calls the Galatians to refrain from abusing their freedom. Instead, they are to serve one another. A very literal translation of "serve one another" can be, "become slaves of one another."

v. 14

"For the ... as yourself"
> cf. Mk. 12:28-31. Liberty does not equal license. We are bound to love.

v. 15

"But if ... one another"
> The Galatians are not to "bite and devour" their fellow brethren. These words connote animalistic behavior which is not suitable for humans, let alone Christians. The ongoing conflict within the Galatian church was rooted in pride and self-righteousness, not love.

CHAPTER 12: THE HOPE OF RIGHTEOUSNESS | *Galatians 5:2-15*

KEY CONCEPTS

CIRCUMCISION

4. Read Acts 16:1-3. What is the difference between Paul's anti-circumcision stance in Galatians and his circumcision of Timothy in Acts 16:1-3?

FREEDOM IN CHRIST

5. How do we avoid using "our freedom as an opportunity for the flesh"? What is Paul calling us to?

6. Read Romans 6:1-4. What principles in this passage guard believers from abusing their freedom?

7. In Mark 12:28-34, Christ tells a scribe that loving God and neighbor are the greatest commandments. How do we practically live according to these mandates?

CHAPTER 12: THE HOPE OF RIGHTEOUSNESS | *Galatians 5:2-15*

APPLICATION

Christianity is not a set of regulations or rules. It is a faith founded upon the person and work of Jesus Christ and the believer's identification with him. In no one else is salvation found; nor is salvation found within ourselves. We can spend all day trying to find an inkling of internal spirituality; but, the revelation of God is not internal, it is external. We cannot save ourselves. Only Jesus can.

As we proceed into the next chapter, may we examine our hearts. Are we serving other believers as God requires of us? Are we bound to our church just as we are bound to our Father? Are we abusing the freedom granted us, or are we using it to pursue holiness?

May we remain in the grace of God, living as one who is perfect in God's sight. There is no other way to live and no other gospel to root ourselves in. Stand firm in this faith and be sure to live it out, lest you find yourself standing on sinking sand (Matt. 7:24-27).

NOTES

CHAPTER 12: THE HOPE OF RIGHTEOUSNESS | *Galatians 5:2-15*

CHAPTER 13:

THE FRUIT OF THE SPIRIT

GALATIANS 5:16-26

SPARK A CONNECTION

1. Do you desire to live a fruitful and faithful life to the Lord but find yourself deterred by the flesh? How does your flesh affect this effort?

_____

_____

_____

_____

2. Even the Apostle Paul struggled against his own fallen flesh. Read Romans 7:13-20, taking note of similarities between your struggle and Paul's.

_____

_____

_____

_____

3. Discuss: There may be fellow believers around you who have experienced the same struggles you have. Share how you have been able to deter the sinful effects of the flesh and walk by the Spirit.

CHAPTER 13: THE FRUIT OF THE SPIRIT | *Galatians 5:16-26*

BACKGROUND AND CONTEXT

Avoiding the temptation of resorting to one's own works to save them and trusting in the justifying power of the cross has been the central theme of Galatians. Now, as we turn to this crucial passage, we learn about the sanctifying power of the Holy Spirit.

The fruit of the Spirit—which inspired the cover of this book!—are the marks of a true believer. These are inner virtues that yield outer reactions. They are contrasted with what we might call the fruits of the flesh, acts of evil that are firmly rooted in our worldly desires.

Look carefully then how you walk, not as unwise but as wise, making the best use of the time, because the days are evil. Therefore do not be foolish, but understand what the will of the Lord is. And do not get drunk with wine, for that is debauchery, but be filled with the Spirit, addressing one another in psalms and hymns and spiritual songs, singing and making melody to the Lord with your heart, giving thanks always and for everything to God the Father in the name of our Lord Jesus Christ, submitting to one another out of reverence for Christ.

- Ephesians 5:15-21

As Paul exhorts the Ephesians to carefully examine their walk, he commands the Galatians to walk by the Spirit. Walking implies a continual movement—a way of life. So, we learn that though the walk of a Christian begins at confession, it does not end there. There are many people who will profess Christ but do not possess Christ. This is the state of the Judaizers, at best. They are teachers who may have an understanding of Christ yet have not received him.

The Apostle James encourages believers to watch their walks and actions in his epistle, for "even the demons believe—and shudder!" (Jas. 2:19b). If we have a head recognition of Christ that is void of a heart recognition, then we have believed in vain, just like the demons of hell. The fruits that emerge from such a false convert are blasphemous and fake, though they may behold some form of power that is Satanically derived, keeping them under delusion (2 Thess. 2:11). This type of punishment is the just reaction of God to the rebellion of humanity.

For although they knew God, they did not honor him as God or give thanks to him, but they became futile in their thinking, and their foolish hearts were darkened. Claiming to be wise, they became fools, and exchanged the glory of the immortal God for images resembling mortal man and birds and animals and creeping things. Therefore God gave them up in the lusts of their

CHAPTER 13: THE FRUIT OF THE SPIRIT | *Galatians 5:16-26*

hearts to impurity, to the dishonoring of their bodies among themselves, because they exchanged the truth about God for a lie and worshiped and served the creature rather than the Creator, who is blessed forever! Amen.

- Romans 1:21-25

In this dark passage in Romans, this group of people is let go of by the hand of God. He turns them over to their own destructive passions: gossip, idolatry, homosexual practices and even murder. These practices are among those Paul says are unfit for believers. They stand in contrast to the working of the Spirit in one's life. Instead, believers are to embody the virtues we will see in the following passage.

PASSAGE

GALATIANS 5:16-26

[16] But I say, walk by the Spirit, and you will not gratify the desires of the flesh. [17] For the desires of the flesh are against the Spirit, and the desires of the Spirit are against the flesh, for these are opposed to each other, to keep you from doing the things you want to do. [18] But if you are led by the Spirit, you are not under the law. [19] Now the works of the flesh are evident: sexual immorality, impurity, sensuality, [20] idolatry, sorcery, enmity, strife, jealousy, fits of anger, rivalries, dissensions, divisions, [21] envy, drunkenness, orgies, and things like these. I warn you, as I warned you before, that those who do such things will not inherit the kingdom of God. [22] But the fruit of the Spirit is love, joy, peace, patience, kindness, goodness, faithfulness, [23] gentleness, self-control; against such things there is no law. [24] And those who belong to Christ Jesus have crucified the flesh with its passions and desires.

[25] If we live by the Spirit, let us also keep in step with the Spirit. [26] Let us not become conceited, provoking one another, envying one another.

INSIGHTS AND EXPOSITION

v. 16

"But I ... the flesh"

The solution to ecclesial conflict and abuse is walking by the Spirit. The Spirit's opposition to the flesh will suppress the desire to do wrong by others.

v. 17

"to keep you from doing the things you want to do"

All Christians have two natures: a sinful nature and a new nature. While the sinful nature may be subdued by the new nature, it will never be completely eradicated until the believer is glorified (Rom. 8:23).

v. 18

"But if ... the law"

Paul summarizes his argument in v. 18. Living in the Spirit is contrary to living by the Law. Christians do not walk a path of legalism, nor a path of license. Instead, they walk a path of love.

vv. 19-21

"Now the works of the flesh are evident"
>1) By this, Paul means that the flesh reaps evidentially sinful fruit. He will contrast these fruits with those of the Spirit. 2) Christ said what comes out of one's heart is what defiles them. These works are simply evidence of an unregenerate heart (Mk. 7:20-23).

"sexual immorality"
>Gr.: *porneia*, all manners of sinful sexual relationships; fornication.

"impurity"
>Gr.: *akatharsia*, moral uncleanliness.

"sensuality"
>Gr.: *aselgia*, licentiousness.

"idolatry"
>Gr.: *eidōlolatria*, worship of idols.

"sorcery"
>Gr.: *pharmakeia*, witchcraft; the use of illicit substances.

CHAPTER 13: THE FRUIT OF THE SPIRIT | *Galatians 5:16-26*

"enmity"

    Gr.: *echthrai*, hostility (used in the plural form denoting hostility between groups).

"strife"

    Gr.: *eris*, discord or contention.

"jealousy"

    Gr.: *zēlos*, jealously; zeal; ardor.

"fits of anger"

    Gr.: *thymoi*, expressions of rage, usually associated with emotions of jealousy.

"rivalries"

    Gr.: *eritheiai*, selfish ambition; attempts to get ahead of others.

"dissensions"

    Gr.: *dichostasia*, separations.

"divisions"

    Gr.: *haireseis*, faction or sect; from the root word, aireō, which means to execute or destroy.

"envy"
> Gr.: *phthonoi*, covetousness; the desire to take what is someone else's.

"drunkenness"
> Gr.: *methai*, excessive use of strong drink.

"orgies"
> Gr.: *kōmoi*, sexual activity in groups. In relation to drunkenness, cultic practices involved drunken orgies as worship to gods.

"and things like these"
> In essence, Paul adds an "etc." at the end of this exhaustive list of sinful fruits.

"will not inherit the kingdom of God"
> Those who live their lives in such a way that these sins become habitual practices prove themselves to be unbelievers. They will not inherit the kingdom of God (cf. 1 Cor. 6:9-10).

vv. 22-23

"But the fruit of the Spirit is"
> Paul now contrasts the fruits of the flesh with holy fruit. The singular use of the word "fruit"

CHAPTER 13: THE FRUIT OF THE SPIRIT | *Galatians 5:16-26*

implies unity among all of the Spirit's fruit. They come as a package deal.

"love"

Gr.: *agapē*, self-sacrificial love. When compared with eros, erotic love, and phileō, brotherly love, agapeō stands out as the noblest kind of love.

"joy"

Gr.: *chara*, inner rejoicing (Jn. 15:11).

"peace"

Gr.: *eirēnē*, inner tranquility and quietness (Jn. 14:27).

"patience"

Gr.: *makrothymia*, forbearance (Col. 1:11).

"kindness"

Gr.: *chrēstotēs*, benevolence (Eph. 2:7).

"goodness"

Gr.: *agatōsynē*, uprightness.

"faithfulness"

Gr.: *pistis*, faith; or, in this context, the quality of being faithful.

"gentleness"

> Gr.: *prautēs*, humility; meekness (2 Tim. 2:25).

"self-control"

> Gr.: *enkrateia*, control over one's action; self-mastery. This word is only used three times in the New Testament (Acts 24:25; 2 Pet. 1:6).

"against such things there is no law"

> These practices are not regulated by God such as the aforementioned fruits of the flesh. They are yielded from one's inner state of righteousness through Christ, not through the external Law, proving them to be a genuine believer.

v. 24

"crucified the flesh"

> Through water baptism and the baptism of the Holy Spirit, every believer has laid aside their sinful natures and taken on a new nature (Jn. 3:5-6; Rom. 6:1-6, 11-12).

vv. 25-26

"If we ... one another"

> Keeping in step with the Spirit will supernaturally suppress our innately sinful desires.

CHAPTER 13: THE FRUIT OF THE SPIRIT | *Galatians 5:16-26*

KEY CONCEPTS

FRUITS OF THE SPIRIT

4. What does walking in the flesh look like?

5. What does walking in the Spirit look like?

6. Read Romans 6:6. Does this text imply that we will no longer struggle with sin? Why or why not?

7. If a believer falls into one of the fleshly sins mentioned in this passage, does that mean they are automatically cast away from the people of God?

8. Read Ephesians 5:1-16. What similarities and differences do you note between Galatians' list and Ephesians'?

APPLICATION

The fruit of the Spirit is a package deal. These various virtues are the united, external results of the inward change that took place when God gave you a new heart. Just as your confession of Christ was rooted in your inward faith, the fruit of the Spirit will bear witness to the Spirit's indwelling of your being.

With this being said, do others see evidence of your belief in Christ through the fruit you bear? Are you marked by love? Joy? Peace? Patience? Kindness? Goodness? Faithfulness? Gentleness? Self-Control? If you are shaky on your answer, then consider praying over this passage. Ask the Lord to make you a ripe tree that is ready to produce the fruit he is calling you to.

NOTES

CHAPTER 13: THE FRUIT OF THE SPIRIT | *Galatians 5:16-26*

CHAPTER 14:

BEAR ONE ANOTHER'S BURDENS

GALATIANS 6:1-18

SPARK A CONNECTION

1. Consider a time in your life when you were not walking faithfully with the Lord. Were you surrounded by other believers who could hold you accountable? Who were they?

2. Be honest with yourself. If you fell into sin tomorrow, would you be willing to submit to the gentle, prayerful and biblical correction of fellow believers?

3. Discuss: If you find yourself struggling to let go of pride and humbly accept the correction of God and his church, share your heart with those around you. Commit to pray for one another and demonstrate accountability as the Lord performs his sanctifying work.

CHAPTER 14: BEAR ONE ANOTHER'S BURDENS | *Galatians 6:1-18*

BACKGROUND AND CONTEXT

Consider this: after your long workday, you decide to go out for a quick grocery run. You don't need much, so you only buy the essentials—eggs, some fruit and a few toiletries. Carrying your exceptionally light load, you casually saunter out of the supermarket, taking note of another shopper walking to their car. This shopper is red-faced, carrying five times the number of bags you have in both hands. These jumbo bags—only used for the fourth of July!—are filled to the brim with various kinds of meat, vegetables, beverage cartons, laundry detergents and more miscellaneous items. Certainly, a heavy load for one person to carry.

So, seeing their struggle, you rush over to this poor shopper. Though you have a few bags of your own to lug, you nevertheless take on the struggler's load, sacrificing your time and energy so they can make it to their car, too.

This image is similar to the one Paul is portraying in this final chapter of Galatians. In the context of the churches—and it is no different now—there were those who were spiritually strong. Their walk was upright, their church participation was sky high and they stood as examples to other believers. Meanwhile, there were others who were not living up to these standards. They found themselves wandering from the truth, thus unable to support the body of Christ, and were the antitheses of Christian character.

In light of these juxtaposed Christians, Paul prepares an exhortation to those who find themselves as the strong ones in this comparison. Though those who are weak have an obligation to live as one for whom Christ died, the apostle understands their frailty. Therefore, in an effort to establish a church that supports members who are in desperate need, he encourages strong believers to carry the burdens of the transgressors among them. This requires self-sacrifice, a level of humility that all Christians are expected and exhorted to maintain. We do not get to pick and choose when we help believers in need.

The Reformer, Martin Luther, once powerfully commented on this subject:

> *"If there is anything in us, it is not our own; it is a gift of God. But if it is a gift of God, then it is entirely a debt one owes to love, that is, to the law of Christ. And if it is a debt owed to love, then I must serve others with it, not myself. Thus my learning is not my own; it belongs to the unlearned and is the debt I owe to them. My chastity is not my own; it belongs to those who commit sins of the flesh, and I am obligated to serve them through it by offering it to God for them, by sustaining and excusing them, and thus with my respectability, veiling their shame before God and man ... Thus my wisdom belongs to the foolish, my power to the oppressed. Thus my wealth belongs to the poor, my righteousness to the sinners ... It is with all these qualities that we must stand before God and intervene on behalf of those who do not have them, as though clothed with someone else's garment ... for this is what Christ did for us."*

CHAPTER 14: BEAR ONE ANOTHER'S BURDENS | *Galatians 6:1-18*

PASSAGE

GALATIANS 6:1-18

¹ Brothers, if anyone is caught in any transgression, you who are spiritual should restore him in a spirit of gentleness. Keep watch on yourself, lest you too be tempted. ² Bear one another's burdens, and so fulfill the law of Christ. ³ For if anyone thinks he is something, when he is nothing, he deceives himself. ⁴ But let each one test his own work, and then his reason to boast will be in himself alone and not in his neighbor. ⁵ For each will have to bear his own load.

⁶ Let the one who is taught the word share all good things with the one who teaches. ⁷ Do not be deceived: God is not mocked, for whatever one sows, that will he also reap. ⁸ For the one who sows to his own flesh will from the flesh reap corruption, but the one who sows to the Spirit will from the Spirit reap eternal life. ⁹ And let us not grow weary of doing good, for in due season we will reap, if we do not give up. ¹⁰ So then, as we have opportunity, let us do good to everyone, and especially to those who are of the household of faith.

¹¹ See with what large letters I am writing to you with my own hand. ¹² It is those who want to make a good showing in the flesh who would force you to be circumcised, and only in order that they may not be persecuted for the cross of Christ. ¹³ For even those who are circumcised do not themselves keep the law, but they desire to have you circumcised that they may boast in your flesh. ¹⁴ But far be it from me to boast except in the cross of our Lord Jesus Christ, by which the world has been crucified to me, and I to the world.

15 For neither circumcision counts for anything, nor uncircumcision, but a new creation. 16 And as for all who walk by this rule, peace and mercy be upon them, and upon the Israel of God.

17 From now on let no one cause me trouble, for I bear on my body the marks of Jesus.

18 The grace of our Lord Jesus Christ be with your spirit, brothers. Amen.

CHAPTER 14: BEAR ONE ANOTHER'S BURDENS | *Galatians 6:1-18*

INSIGHTS AND EXPOSITION

v. 1

"Brothers"

Paul addresses the Galatians as siblings in Christ. He expects them to live a life of loving service, not law-keeping for the sake of righteousness.

"if anyone ... of gentleness"

1) Those who are walking in the Spirit are to help believers caught in sin by leading them toward faithful living. This is contrary to the way the Jewish leaders treated the woman caught in adultery (Jn. 8:3-5). 2) "Restore," Gr.: *katartizete*, to mend or repair.

"Keep watch"

Gr.: *skopeō*, to look out for. This is a strong, emphatic verb.

v. 2

"Bear one ... of Christ"

Bearing a burden connotes carrying something for the long haul. This is the manner in which believers are to look out for one another. Doing so will fulfill the law of Christ (Gal. 5:14).

vv. 3-5

"let each one test his own work"
> "Test," Gr.: *dokimazetō*, to examine, test or approve (1 Pet. 1:7).

"then his reason to boast will be in himself and not his neighbor"
> This does not mean believers should glory in themselves (Rom. 12:3). Paul is commanding the Galatians to refrain from comparing themselves to one another and to look only upon what God has done in their individual lives.

"For each will have to bear his own load"
> Paul is not contradicting himself here. "Load" does not refer to burdens, as in v. 2. Rather, it refers to a believer's responsibility to live life fruitfully.

v. 6

"good things"
> This does not seem to refer to monetary gifts as in 1 Cor. 9:7-14. The good things Paul is speaking of seem to be morally good actions or teachings.

CHAPTER 14: BEAR ONE ANOTHER'S BURDENS | *Galatians 6:1-18*

vv. 7-8

"Do not be deceived"

> Here, "deceived" is derived from *planaō*, which means to lead atray. Paul does not desire for them to become bewitched concerning another point altogether.

"for whatever ... also reap"

> The agricultural practice of sowing and reaping is brought to light. If you sow sin, then do not expect to reap something different later (Num. 32:23).

vv. 9-10

"And let us not grow weary of doing good"

> Believers should remain steadfast and immovable in their care for others (Heb. 12:1-3).

"as we have opportunity"

> "Opportunity" is translated from *kairos*, a fixed time period.

v. 11

"large letters"

Paul seems to have written in block letters as if writing a public notice. This was not the ordinary way to draft a letter. If this theory is true, then the large letters serve his rhetorical purpose. A second option has to do with Paul's poor eyesight (Gal. 4:13-15). It is a possibility that Paul had to write with large letters since his vision was impaired.

"with my own hand"

Paul wrote this letter himself as opposed to dictating it to a scribe (1 Cor. 16:21; Col. 4:18; 2 Thess. 3:17).

vv. 12-13

"It is those who want to make a good showing in the flesh"

Paul's central assertion in these two verses is that the Judaizers simply want to boast over increasing numbers in their fold; yet, even these pro-Law teachers do not keep the Law themselves. The flesh is opposed to the Spirit, so the Judaizers' supposed ministry is in vain (Lk. 16:14-15).

v. 14

"But far .. the world"

> 1) The conjunction "But" denotes a contrast between the way of the Judaizers and the way of Paul. 2) Paul's boasting here is like that of v. 4. This is a type of boasting performed in a righteous manner (e.g. exulting in the Lord), rather than a prideful manner. 3) Paul has been crucified to the "world." The "world" here is *kosmos*, which refers to the entire universe. Paul seems to be referring to the *kosmos* in a spiritual sense, though, which would then indicate that this world is full of all types of transgression and sin that he no longer regards.

v. 15

"For neither ... new creation"

> Summarizing the letter's central assertion, Paul reiterates that circumcision of the flesh means nothing. What matters is a circumcision of the heart, which is a factor in the new inner-person (Deut. 10:16; 2 Cor. 5:17).

v. 16

"the Israel of God"
> This group is the second set of people mentioned in v. 16, indicating that "the Israel of God" may in fact be Jewish believers. These Jews are the true descendants of Abraham (Rom. 9:6-7).

v. 17

"I bear on my body the marks of Jesus"
> cf. 2 Cor. 11:24-25.

v. 18

"The grace ... Amen"
> Paul concludes the letter similarly to how he began: with the grace of God. He calls the Galatians, "brothers," ending on a heartfelt and tender appeal.

CHAPTER 14: BEAR ONE ANOTHER'S BURDENS | *Galatians 6:1-18*

KEY CONCEPTS

BEARING ONE ANOTHER'S BURDENS

4. What does bearing one another's burdens look like?

5. What does Paul mean when he writes, "For each will have to bear his own load?" Is he contradicting himself?

SOWING AND REAPING

6. What is the concept of sowing and reaping (vv. 7-9)?

THE MESSAGE OF GALATIANS

7. Now having read and studied the book of Galatians, how would you describe its central message?

8. Write down a few key takeaways that you would like to intentionally apply to your life.

CHAPTER 14: BEAR ONE ANOTHER'S BURDENS | *Galatians 6:1-18*

APPLICATION

As we have learned through our study of Paul's letter, your law-keeping is worthless. You do not contribute to your own righteousness. If your salvation was dependent upon you, then you would be accursed. But because Christ came to live a perfect life on our behalf, we now have access to new life. This new life is characterized by internal holiness only seen by God, not external displays seen by all. Your righteous deeds proceed from the fountain of your heart, which God has redeemed to show his glory in this fallen world.

As you conclude your study, I would like to ask you to consider writing the names of fellow believers who can carry your burdens. There may be stumbling blocks down the road that will cause you to stumble. But if you are plugged into a local body of believers who love you and care for you, then you can rely on your brothers and sisters in Christ to pick you up when you fall down. Likewise, write the names of believers whom you would like to support. You never know who may be in need of a helping hand.

_____

_____

_____

_____

_____

_____

NOTES

CHAPTER 14: BEAR ONE ANOTHER'S BURDENS | *Galatians 6:1-18*

BIBLIOGRAPHY

Barry, John D. *The Lexham Bible Dictionary*. Lexham Press, 2016.

Boice, James Montgomery. *The Expositor's Bible Commentary: Romans - Galatians*. Edited by Gæbelein E. Frank, vol. 10, Zondervan Publishing House, 1976.

Calvin, John. *Calvin's New Testament Commentaries, Volume 11: Galatians, Ephesians, Philippians, and Colossians*. Wm. B. Eerdmans-Lightning Source, 1996.

Cousar, Charles. *Galatians: Interpretation: A Bible Commentary for Teaching and Preaching*. Reprint, Louisville, Kentucky, Westminster John Knox Press, 2012.

Jamieson, Robert, et al. *Commentary Critical and Explanatory on the Whole Bible*. Zondervan Publishing House, 1934.

Luther, Martin. *Galatians (Crossway Classic Commentaries)*. Crossway; First Thus edition (1998–05-11), 1998.

MacArthur, John. *The MacArthur New Testament Commentary: Galatians (Volume 19)*. Moody Publishers, 1987.

Moo, Douglas, et al. *Galatians (Baker Exegetical Commentary on the New Testament)*. e-book, Baker Academic, 2013.

Piper, John. *Why I Love the Apostle Paul: 30 Reasons*. Crossway, 2019.

Piper, John. *21 Servants of Sovereign Joy: Faithful, Flawed, and Fruitful*. Crossway, 2018.

Walvoord, John, and Roy Zuck. *The Bible Knowledge Commentary Acts and Epistles (BK Commentary)*. David C Cook, 2018.

Wenham, Gordon, et al. *New Bible Commentary (The New Bible Set)*. 21st Century, e-book, IVP Academic, 1994.

Wright, N. T., and Michael Bird. *The New Testament in Its World: An Introduction to the History, Literature, and Theology of the First Christians.* Illustrated, Zondervan Academic, 2019.

Yoon, David I. "Identifying the End of Paul's Speech to Peter in Galatians 2 : Register Analysis as a Heuristic Tool." Filología Neotestamentaria, vol. 28–29, no. 48–49, Jan. 2016, pp. 57–79.

CPSIA information can be obtained
at www.ICGtesting.com
Printed in the USA
BVHW051233041122
651158BV00004B/818